Rolf Goetz

Madeira

50 selected valley and mountain walks

With 84 colour photographs,
50 1:25.000 / 1:50.000 walking maps
and a 1:250.000 overview map

ROTHER · MUNICH

Front cover:
The Levada 25 Fontes is one of Madeira's finest walks.

Frontispiece (photo on page 2):
Sheer coastal cliffs give the São Lourenço peninsula a primeval feel.

All photographs are by the author, with the exception of the photos on pages 26, 139 Sabine Gebauer; 9, 12 l., 13, 15, 64, 96, 123, 141, 143 Werner Gottwald.

Cartography:
Walking maps to a scale of 1:25.000 / 1:50.000, © Freytag-Berndt, Vienna (adapetd by Kartographie Christian Rolle, Holzkirchen); Overview maps with a scale of 1:250.000 / 1:370.000, © Bergverlag Rother GmbH (drawn by Kartographie Christian Rolle, Holzkirchen)

Translation:
Gill Round

1st edition 2001
© Bergverlag Rother GmbH, Munich
ISBN 3-7633-4811-5

Distributed in Great Britain by Cordee, 3a De Montfort Street, Leicester Great Britain LE1 7HD, www.cordee.co.uk
in USA by AlpenBooks, 3616 South Road, C-1, Mukilteo, WA 98275 USA, www.alpenbooks.com

Preface

Every island has its own cliché and Madeira is synonymous with a fortified wine which although it may have peaked in its popularity, is valued by connoisseurs as much now as ever before. The all-year-round mild climate has resulted in Madeira's elaborate nickname 'floating island of flowers in the Atlantic'. The Bird of Paradise Flower and Torch Lilies, Lilies of the Nyle and Hydrangeas prove beyond doubt that Madeira is blessed with a magnificent display of flowers like no other island. And this Atlantic beauty has quietly blossomed into an extra special walkers' paradise.

The first word that walkers might learn in Portuguese is 'levada'. Levada walking is unique to Madeira. Narrow irrigation channels cover the whole of the island in a cleverly devised network. Without too much change in elevation you can discover some of the remotest corners on Madeira on the maintenance paths beside the channels. A good half of the walks in this guide are levada walks. They lead you through fertile farmland with sugar cane, banana trees and vines, past terraces skillfully moulded into the craggy island topography, awakening associations with Bali or the Phillipines. The paths pass rushing waterfalls and gorges, precipitous cliffs and marshy high moors. The subtropical vegetation of laurel forests and heathland in the still unspoiled valleys of the north is sometimes so luxuriant, it's as if you are walking through an emerald green tunnel.

With all the fascination of the levada paths you should not forget, however, that this volcanic island is also an excellent area for mountain walkers. The almost 1900m high central massif has walks for everyone. The three summit walk from Arieiro over the Torres up to Pico Ruivo seems decidedly alpine. The section spectacularly cut into the rock is considered to be a particularly outstanding walk, with justification. Together with remote shepherds' paths and adventurous coastal paths there are the so-called 'veredas', old linking paths which, up to a few decades ago, were the only approach to isolated villages. A typical feature is the rounded steps of the cobbled paths which Madeiran people fondly call 'ox-foot cobbles'.

The modern age hasn't spared Madeira either and the network of paths can change due to new forest paths, roads, the building of houses and last but not least, the ever-changing processes of nature itself. If you find changes on your walks please inform the publishers. It only remains for me to wish you some invigorating and enjoyable days on the 'floating island of flowers in the Atlantic'.

Rolf Goetz

Contents

Tourist Information

Use of the Guide
Each route description is prefaced by an overview of the most important information in dossier-like form. The line of the route is marked on the coloured walking map. All destinations, locations, starting and base points, as well as each main stage destination can be found in the index. The location of each walk is shown on the overview maps.

Grade
Most of the walks go along clear paths and tracks. However this should not detract from the fact that some walks demand a strong physical condition, sure-footedness, a head for heights and orientation skills. You should also take into consideration that the difficulties might increase after periods of bad weather. To help you judge the grade of the suggested routes more easily, the route numbers are colour-coded as follows:

BLUE
These routes are usually comfortably broad and only moderately steep, so that they can be undertaken with relatively little danger, even in poor weather.
They can normally be safely undertaken by children and older people.

RED
These mountain paths are mainly narrow and can be quite exposed in short sections.
They should, therefore, only be undertaken by sure-footed mountain walkers. Some short sections can require good route-finding ability and a good head for heights.

BLACK
These mountain paths and mule tracks are frequently narrow and steep. In places they can be very exposed and traverses can lead over scree slopes or sliding sections. In some cases you might need to use your hands. Levada paths can be very precipitous.
These walks should only be attempted if you have a good head for heights, are sure-footed, fit and an experienced mountain walker with good route-finding ability.

Getting there
You can reach most of the walks described in this guide by public transport. You will find a bus time-table with the most useful services for walkers on page 18/19. Some locations require a car.

The tunnel to the Folhadal.

Walking times
The time details refer to real walking time and do not take into account stops and photo opportunities. The times for each stage of the walk and the total time is given.

Equipment
All walks, apart from a few easy ones along the levadas, require you to wear stout walking shoes with good soles. You should also take with you plenty of water, rain and sun protection and a warm pullover for cooler days. A good torch is also necessary for the numerous tunnels.

Dangers
Most walks follow clear paths. Special mention is given to areas without paths, sections of climbing or where you need a good head for heights. There might be landslides at heights above 800m and clouds can suddenly form, making many mountain and levada paths temporarily impassable.

Best season
Madeira is ideal for walking all year round. The summer months are not all that hot and the winter months are mild with, for middle Europeans,

spring-like weather. June until the beginning of September guarantee the most stable weather conditions with only moderate precipitation on the north side. In winter you should be prepared for cool and rainy weather in the north and in areas above 600m. It can be cold and might occasionally snow in the high mountains.

In contrast, the south side of the island is usually dry and mild even in winter.

The sea-water pool in Porto Moniz –
fishermen come here when the swimmers have left.

Refreshment and accommodation

In the mountains there are a handful of state-owned huts but only the Casa do Abrigo do Pico Ruivo has a warden. It offers the simplest accommodation by prior booking. Send a letter of reservation to Regiáo Autonoma da Madeira, Secretaria Regional de Agricultura, Florestas e Pescas, 9000 Funchal. The tourist office in Funchal can provide further help. If you send them the dates you wish to stay you will receive written confirmation to show to the warden. It's recommended that you book early for weekends in summer since there are a lot of Portuguese walkers also making use of the free overnight accommodation. There are snack-bars and restaurants along some of the walks.

Maps and guides

The road map of Madeira 1:50.000 by Freytag & Berndt is recommended. A useful topographical map (2 sheets) with a scale of 1:50.000 is published by the Instituto Geográfico e Cadastral. Very detailed but rather antiquated is the Carta Militar de Portugal for Madeira, to a scale of 1:25.000 (9 sheets). Both topographical maps are difficult to obtain while you are there so it's best to order them from a travel bookshop at home. *Madeira*, an illustrated identification guide for those interested in botany, by António da Costa and Luis Franquinho, is obtainable from tourist offices and souvenir shops in Madeira.

Tips for one-way and long distance walks

Some walks are conceived as one-way day walks where the destination is a long way from the starting point. You are therefore advised either to take advantage of public transport (bus, taxi), go on an organised trip or join forces with another walker with a car. The best solution is to park a car at your destination before you leave for the walk.

Long distance walkers can cross the island from Funchal on a multi-day levada walk as far as Porto da Cruz. The individual stages Monte – Camacha – Santo António da Serra – Portela – Porto da Cruz are fully described in this guide. Allow two or three days for this walk and stop overnight in Camacha, Santo António da Serra and Porto da Cruz. A two-day crossing of the central massif from Santana via Pico das Pedras, Pico Ruivo and Pico do Arieiro is also possible and then descend to Funchal. You can stay overnight in the Pico Ruivo mountain hut (only by prior booking) and at Pico do Arieiro.

Walking on Madeira

The main island of the Madeira archipelago lies geographically nearer to Africa than to Europe. Whilst it's almost 900km from its Portuguese motherland, it's only 500km from the Moroccan coast and 400km from the Canary Islands further south. About 270 000 inhabitants live on a surface area of 741 sq. km, with almost half of them in the densely populated area of the capital, Funchal.

In spite of its manageable size Madeira offers a diverse landscape. The island rose up out of the Atlantic through volcanic activity 20 million years ago and is dominated by a strangely weather-beaten mountain range whose highest peak is the 1862m high Pico Ruivo.

There are hardly any beaches on Madeira which is strange for an island. Only a few shingle and pebble beaches provide relief from the steep coastline which drops away precipitously into the sea. The people of Madeira manage with sea-water pools which you can find in almost every town of reasonable size. If you are interested in golden yellow sandy beaches then you will need to make the 15 minute flight to the neighbouring island of Porto Santo to find one.

Flora and fauna

Except for the dry São Lourenço peninsula in the east, Madeira does credit to its nickname of the 'floating island of flowers in the Atlantic'. Indigenous plants and imports from the tropics ensure that there's a splendid array of flowers all year round, incomparable in Europe. When Portuguese discoverers took possession of the island in the 15th century, they christened it the 'island of woods' (Portuguese madeira = wood). Clear-felling considerably reduced the areas of forests and the remains of evergreen laurel forests

The Hydrangea is a typical feature of Madeira's levadas.
Palm ferns from South Africa are the pride of the botanical gardens.

only survived in the gorges where access was difficult. The relics of the Tertiary period play a very important role in the island's water balance.

The Llily-of-the-valley tree belongs to the plant community of the laurel woods as well as Stinklaurel, Azores laurel, Madeira mahogany and ferns, Sow thistles and a lot more besides make up the richly varied undergrowth.

The endemic Madeira lizard.

The mountains are covered in low forests of tree heathers, the gnarled trunks of which can be found almost up to the high mountain summit region.

Star of the endemic plant world is the pride of Madeira shrub (Echium candicans) which produces magnificent mauve candle-like blossoms in summer.

The ancient looking Dragon tree with its bizarre branches has become rare.

Compared with the richly varied flora, the range of fauna is quite modest. Except for pets there are no big land mammals. Walkers need have no fear of snakes – they had as little success in making the jump over to this remote island as scorpions and other poisonous animals. If there's a rustling in the bushes it's more likely to be a harmless lizard or a gecko.

The offshore rocky islands are an important refuge for sea birds like the Yellow-beaked Cory's Shearwater and the Madeiran Storm petrel. Only on Madeira can you find Madeira-Sardinella and a wood pigeon which lives in laurel woods.

On the Desertas islands there are still a few Monk seals. These animals, threatened with extinction, also used to inhabit the coasts of the main island in great numbers.

The most important fish is the Scabbardfish (Portuguese espada), a Madeiran delicacy which is caught with long lines in depths of up to 2000m.

Nature parks and botanical gardens

Large surface areas above the settlement boundary of 700m are declared nature parks. The laurel wood in the Parque Forestal of Ribeiro Frio (walks 18, 19 and 20) and the Parque da Queimadas (walks 25 and 26) enjoy special protection. Both lie at about 900m up in the highest precipitation regions of the island which accounts for the luxuriant vegetation comparable to sub-tropical mountain forests.

Besides nature parks Madeira can offer interesting botanical gardens which are well worth a visit. The English brought the art of horticulture to the is-

Bananas thrive well in the sub-tropical climate on the south coast.

land. Sub-tropical and tropical plants from all continents find ideal growing conditions here thanks to the all-year-round mild climate.

Together with a section of endemic plants like the Dragon tree, the *Jardim Botânico da Madeira* in Funchal houses exotic species from all over the world, amongst them some useful plants like coffee, cinnamon and vanilla. There's a bird sanctuary and a very beautiful orchid garden connected to the botanical garden.

Perhaps even more attractive is the *Quinta do Palheiro Ferreiro*. Also known as *Blandy's Garden* it is famous for its old tree stock and the magnificent southern African Proteaceae and Camelias.

Highlight amongst the gardens is the *Monte Palace Tropical Park*. It has a stately collection of palm ferns. Sumptuous ornamental plants under shady sequoias and tree ferns are a feast for the eyes.

Environment and ecology

The luxuriant vegetation and magnificent flowers cannot hide the fact that Madeira has substantial ecological problems too. The high density of population leads to the regions close to the coast, especially in the south, becoming overdeveloped. Compared to the Canary islands of about the same size, Lanzarote and La Palma, almost three times as many people live on Madeira.

As a result of the high level of population there is a corresponding pressure for road development. With the subsidy from the EU, Madeira is seeking to achieve European standards. In spite of the fissured topography fast roads and motorways eat their way ruthlessly through the island. Valleys are bridged and tunnels are cut through the mountain ridges. Many an old paved path has fallen victim to a new road.

One problem which cannot escape your notice is the waste disposal. The change-over to a modern age of packaging happened all too quickly and an environmental awareness was slow to develop. Illegal rubbish tips litter the island and sometimes even levadas are used for quick and easy disposal.

It's to be hoped that environmental education in schools, initiated by the island's government, will have some success with the younger generation.

Levadas

With the levadas Madeira has a unique network of paths for walkers. The irrigation channels were constructed shortly after the island was inhabited in the 15th century to make use of the rich water resources in the island's interior for the cultivation of sugar cane and wine. The construction was dangerous and took many lives. Workers were suspended in wicker baskets from the top of sheer rock faces and channels were hewn with picks out of the rock. Over the course of generations a channel system has evolved today of 1400km in length.

The levadas are 20 to 120cm wide and up to one metre deep. The paths along the levadas serve not only for maintenance, but provide ideal hiking paths at the same time. Apart from some steep ascents and descents to the levadas, they themselves run across the whole of the island with little difference in height. As long as they are sufficiently well-protected you can walk quite comfortably on or next to the little channel walls. As an additional attraction, workers have planted ornamental plants along the edge of the paths – two characteristic ones are Hydrangeas and Lilies of the Nyle which border the paths for many kilometres.

The levadas suit the topographical conditions perfectly.

Information and Addresses

Getting there
You can fly direct to Madeira with numerous charter flights from all the main airports in Great Britain. The Portuguese airline TAP is offering scheduled flights via Lisbon. Flight duration is approximately 4 hours.

Information
In Great Britain: Portuguese Trade an Tourism Office, 22-25a Sackville St., London WIX IDE, tel 020/74941441.

In Madeira: Direcçao Regional de Turismo, Avenida Arriaga 18, 9000 Funchal, tel 291225658.
On the internet: www.madinfo.pt/organismos/madeira

Camping
The only official campsite (Parque de Campismo) is in Porto Moniz, tel 291853447. Wild camping is not publicised, but it is tolerated.

Climate
Madeira has a sub-tropical climate with mild temperatures all year round. The Passat wind gives the island a distinctive microclimate The mountain range in the centre of the island has the effect of a meteorological divide and separates the island into a frequently overcast northern side with high precipitation and a drier and sunnier south. The temperatures between summer and winter vary only a few degrees. Funchal in particular has a favourable climate. The weather on high ground in winter can be changeable and cool.

Emergency
The central emergency number for the police, fire-brigade and ambulance is 112.

FUNCHAL CLIMATE													
Month		1	2	3	4	5	6	7	8	9	10	11	12
Day	°C	16	16	17	20	24	27	29	29	27	23	21	17
Night	°C	9	9	10	12	15	19	21	22	19	16	13	11
Water	°C	16	15	16	16	19	22	24	25	24	23	20	17
sunshine/day	hrs	3	5	6	8	10	12	13	12	10	6	6	4
Days of rain		12	7	8	4	2	1	0	0	2	6	6	10

Safety
Madeira is a safe place for your travels. Crimes of violence are rare and petty theft is also less frequent than in middle Europe.

Language
Portuguese is spoken on Madeira, but you will easily get by in the tourist centres with English.

Telephone
The dialling code to Portugal/Madeira is 00351. From Madeira to Great Britain it is 0044.

Accommodation
Madeira has accommodation to suit everyone's pocket. The centre of tourism is Funchal's hotel quarter with many elegant four and five-star luxury hotels. In the old town there are some simple guesthouses. It's also nice to stay in the so-called Quintas, country hotels which are surrounded by tropical gardens. The two state-run Pousadas on the Pico do Arieiro and in Serra de Água are ideal for mountain walkers (centre for reservations, tel 921765658) – you can practically start your walk from right outside the hotel.

Weather forecast
There is up-to-the-minute weather data and a three-day forecast on the internet: www.weatheronline.co.uk

Transport
Bus: From Funchal there are good services to all parts of the island although in the north and the west you need to take into account the long journey times (eg. 2 hours to Santana and over 3 hours to Porto Moniz). There is no central bus station in Funchal and each of the six private bus companies starts from various stops on the Avenida do Mar. A sketch-map with the departure points is available from the Tourist Office of Funchal.

Taxi: There are only taxi ranks in the main resorts. Cross island journeys are made without a taximeter, but according to fixed prices.

Hire car: Rental cars are reasonably priced. A reliable firm is Magos Car in Caniço, tel 291934818, and you can arrange to collect your car at the airport. The driver must be at least 21 years old. Some driving experience is required for the often very narrow and windy mountain roads, added to which Madeiran people's hazardous style of driving takes some getting used to.

TIMETABLES OF THE MOST USEFUL BUS ROUTES

3 Funchal – Estreito de Câmara de Lobos

Mon–Fri 10.30, 12.00, 12.45, 15.05, 16.00, 16.40, 18.15, 19.15
Sat 14.45, 17.35, 18.00, 18.45
Sun 14.05, 17.00
return:
Mon–Fri 6.45, 7.15, 8.00, 8.15, 11.30, 13.05, 14.00, 17.00, 24.00
Sat 7.00, 8.15, 15.05, 15.40, 24.00

6 Funchal – Boaventura (via Encumeada)

daily 7.35, 13.35 (except Sun), 17.30
return:
daily 6.00, 7.15 (except Sun), 15.00

7 Funchal – Ribeira Brava

Mon–Fri 6.45, 9.30, 10.50, 15.30, 17.00, 18.00, 18.30 (except 31.12.), 20.15,
22.30, 23.30
Sat 6.45, 10.50, 13.30, 15.30, 17.00, 20.15, 23.30
Sun 10.05, 12.05, 13.30, 15.30, 17.00, 20.15, 23.30
return:
Mon–Fri 6.05, 8.15, 9.00, 11.00, 12.35, 17.15, 18.35, 19.00, 22.10
Sat 6.05, 8.15, 11.00, 12.30, 15.30, 17.15, 18.35, 22.10
Sun 6.05, 11.45, 13.35, 15.30, 17.15, 18.35, 22.10

29 Funchal – Camacha

daily between 8.00 and 22.00 every 30–60 min.
return:
daily between 7.00 and 19.45 every 30–60 min.

53 Funchal – Faial (via Airport + Portela)

Mon–Fri 10.00, 13.00, 16.15, 18.10 (as far as Porto da Cruz), 19.15
Sat 10.00, 13.00, 15.00
Sun 18.15
return:
Mon–Fri 5.45, 7.45, 10.00, 13.00, 15.30, 17.00, 18.15 (from Porto da Cruz)
Sat 10.00, 15.30, 17.00, 18.15 (from Porto da Cruz)
Sun 10.00, 13.30, 18.15 (from Porto da Cruz)

77 Funchal – Santo António da Serra (via Camacha + Sítio Quatro Estradas)

Mon–Fri 7.35, 10.30, 14.00, 16.30, 18.00, 19.15
Sat 7.35, 10.30, 14.00, 16.30, 19.00
Sun 8.30, 10.30, 14.00, 16.30, 19.15
return:
Mon–Fri 6.30 (via Boqueirão), 7.15, 9.00, 12.00, 16.15, 18.00, 20.30
Sat 7.15, 9.00, 16.15, 18.00
Sun 7.00, 10.00, 12.00, 16.15, 18.00

80/139 Funchal – Porto Moniz

daily 9.00 (via São Vicente)
return:
daily 5.00 (except Sun, via São Vicente), 16.00 (via Ponta do Pargo)

81 Funchal – Curral das Freiras

Mon–Fri 7.35, 8.45, 10.30, 11.30, 13.15, 15.05, 16.30, 18.30, 19.30, 20.30, 21.45,
23.45
Sat 7.40, 8.45, 10.30, 11.30, 13.15, 16.30, 19.30, 21.45, 23.45
Sun 6.40, 9.05, 11.40, 13.15, 16.30, 19.30, 21.45, 23.45
return:
Mon–Fri 6.40, 7.30, 8.45, 10.00, 11.45, 13.15, 14.30, 16.15, 17.45, 19.30, 20.30, 21.30
Sat 6.30, 8.45, 10.00, 12.00, 13.15, 14.30, 17.45, 20.30
Sun 7.40, 10.30, 12.50, 14.30, 17.45, 20.30

96 Funchal – Jardim da Serra (Corticeiras)

daily between 7.00 and 21.00 every 30–60 min. (Sa + So every 1–2 hrs)
return:
daily between 5.00 and 20.00 every 30–60 min.

103 Funchal – Boaventura (via Faial + Santana)

daily 7.15, 13.30 (except Sun + 25./26.12), 16.00 (except Sun + 25./26.12), 18.00
return:
daily 5.30 (except Sun), 7.00, 12.00 (except Sun), 16.00

113 Funchal – Caniçal (via Airport)

Mon–Fri 7.30, 8.30, 9.00, 12.15, 14.30, 15.30, 17.15, 19.30
Sat 7.30, 9.00, 12.15, 14.30, 15.30, 17.15
Sun 7.30, 9.00, 12.15, 15.00, 19.00
return:
Mon–Fri 5.45, 6.45, 7.30, 8.30, 9.30, 10.30, 11.45, 13.10, 14.10, 17.10, 18.10,
19.45
Sat 6.45, 9.30, 10.30, 11.45, 13.10, 14.10, 17.10, 18.10, 19.45, 21.00
Sun 6.45, 9.30, 10.30, 14.10, 17.10, 19.10, 21.00

132 Santana – São Vicente

Mon–Sat 6.00
Sun 8.45
return:
Mon–Sat 10.30, 17.00
Sun 15.00

148 Funchal – Boa Morte

Mon–Sat 13.05
return:
Mon–Sat 6.30, 14.30

156 Funchal – Maroços (via Machico)

Mon–Fri 6.45, 8.00, 10.30, 11.45, 13.15, 16.00, 17.30, 17.45, 19.20, 23.45
Sat 6.45, 8.00, 10.30, 11.45, 13.45, 16.00, 17.45, 19.00, 20.30, 23.45
Sun 10.30, 11.45, 17.45, 20.00, 21.30, 23.45
return:
Mon–Fri 5.45, 6.15, 6.45, 7.30, 8.15, 9.45, 11.30, 12.30, 13.40, 15.30, 18.10, 19.00
Sat 5.45, 6.15, 6.45, 7.30, 11.30, 12.30, 13.10, 15.30
Sun 5.45, 8.15, 11.30, 13.00, 15.45, 20.00, 22.30

NB: no buses on 25.12.

Ponta
do Tristão

Porto Moniz

Santa
EN 101
Lamaceiros

Ribeira da Janela

Achadas
da Cruz

Seixal

Lombada Velha

**Ponta
Delgada**

49

EN 101

*Ponta
do Pargo*

**Ponta
do Pargo**

Sra. do Amparo
Lombada dos
Marinheiros

50

Ribeira da Janela

Parque Natural de Madeira

Pico Ruivo
do Paúl
1640

**São
Vicente**

EN 104
Ginjas

Boaventu

EN

Achada
da Madeira

EN 101

Loural
Vargem

Par

**Fajá da
Ovelha**

48

Raposeira

EN 110

46

Pico Casa
1725

45

Boca da
Encumeada
1007

37

**Paúl
do Mar**

Prazeres

Rabaçal

44

Paúl da Serra

39

EN 110

38

Pic
Gra
165

47

43

36

**Jardim
do Mar**

Estreito da Calheta

42

41

35

34

Calheta

Loreto

Arco da
Calheta

EN 209

**Serra
de Água**

5

EN 104

**Cur
das Freir**

EN 222

7

33

**Madalena
do Mar**

Canhas

6

4

EN 101

EN 222

Tabúa

3

EN 229

**Estreito
de Câm
de Lobo**

Ponta do Sol

**Ribeira
Brava**

Campanário

Quinta
Grande

2

EN 22

Cabo Girão
580

**Câmara
de Lobos**

0 ————————— 10 km

1 : 250 000

Funchal and the south coast

With 120 000 inhabitants **Funchal** is the undisputed island metropolis of Madeira. In spite of an urban life style the town is a good location for walkers with its perfect tourist infra-structure and favourable climate. In addition to the walks in the south you can easily reach the east coast, Curral das Freiras and the central massif.

Funchal became a popular holiday resort for well-off English people over 100 years ago. Opened in 1891, Hotel Reid's is an institution and still today one of the world's most beautiful luxury hotels.

Take a stroll through the old town and visit the botanical garden and the Mercado dos Lavradores overflowing with fruit and vegetables. If you should be on Madeira over New Year the firework display in Funchal is world famous and attracts lots of cruise ships.

The main tourist attraction is a ride in a carros de cesto (wicker basket toboggan), the original form of local transport on the island. It starts from in front of the pilgrims' church in the exclusive residential district of **Monte**, situated at a height of 500m. The vehicle, made from willow twigs woven together, has wooden runners and is steered by two sledge drivers down the 4km long descent to Funchal.

A rewarding stroll – the market hall of Funchal displays a feast for the eyes and the palate.

The sea of houses in Funchal stretches far around the wide-sweeping bay like seats in an amphitheatre.

Câmara de Lobos has almost merged with Funchal. This delightful little fishing village was one of the first settlements on Madeira. The scabbardfish is caught from small boats and cat sharks hang on racks to dry in the sun. The most famous guest in Câmara de Lobos was Sir Winston Churchill. He used to paint up on the view point named after him above the harbour. With a fat cigar in the corner of his mouth he would sit at his easel and capture on canvas the picturesque scene below.

But the picturesque activities in the harbour do not blind you to the obvious poverty of the inhabitants. The outdated fishing fleet has been unable to compete with the modern equipment of foreign fishing cutters for some time now. Alcoholism, hard drugs and child beggars bear witness to the social decline of the place.

An alternative base to Funchal with its characteristic city feel is **Ribeira Brava** at the estuary of the river of the same name. This sun-kissed town offers a handful of middle-class hotels aimed at independent travellers. The accommodation is also used by English and German travel companies. The town is relatively well-placed for the walking areas of Paúl da Serra and Rabaçal. The symbol of Ribeira Brava is the chequer-tiled tower of the parish church São Bento.

1   From Funchal into the Socorridos valley

Along the 'town Levada' to the Levada do Curral

Funchal – Quebradas – Pinheiro das Voltas – Fajã – Pinheiro das Voltas

Starting point: from the old town of Funchal take the No. 45 local bus to the Estádio dos Barreiros and get off above the stadium. Go back along the road 20m from the bus stop and you'll see some steps leading to the Levada dos Piornais. If you are staying in the hotel quarter go from Hotel Reid's along the Estrada Monumental into town and at the Hotel Quinta do Sol turn into the Rua do Dr. Pita. Go next left into Rua da Casa Branca, then up the narrow street on the right (Ladeira da Casa Branca). This meets the Caminho da Nazare in front of the Barreiros stadium. Go left here and down a few steps to the Levada dos Piornais (about 10 minutes from Hotel Reid's).

Return: with No. 16A local bus from Pinheiro das Voltas.

Walking time: Barreiros stadium – Amparo ½ hr, Amparo – Quebradas ½ hr, Quebradas – Pinheiro das Voltas 1 hr, Pinheio das Voltas – Fajã 1 hr, Fajã – Pinheiro das Voltas 1 hr. Total time without detour 4 hrs, with detour 5 hrs.

Ascent: 150m.

Grade: an easy levada walk as far as Quebradas (watch out for holes in the concrete slabs). You need a good head for heights for the detour and the continuation along the 150m higher Levada do Curral.

Refreshment: the snack-bar in Pinheiro das Voltas.

The *Levada dos Piornais* has been bringing water into the capital for 400 years. It serves not only to irrigate the fields and drive the water wheels, but also as the 'laundry room' for residents, as you can see by the number of washing places along the channels. This walk is most suitable for people walking for the first time along a levada. The walk is very popular because you can start from the middle of Funchal.

From the Caminho da Nazare above the **Barreiros stadium** go first upstream along the narrow Levada wall. The capital is already quite rural here and banana plantations reach right up to the hotel area. Vineyards, house gardens with aloes and winter-blossoming poinsettias brighten up the rather sad-looking suburb. Cross over a road and a levada crossing place and you can soon see the Lido swimming pool below. The Cabo Girão rises up ahead out of the sea.

Cross over two asphalt roads in **Amparo** and up on a hill on the right you can see the tower of the village church. Cross over another road in **Quebradas** and the levada disappears under a cobbled road just after the bus stop for the No. 2 local bus. Follow the road for 150m and reach the levada again via some steps. 3 minutes later you meet another road which you follow up right for 5m, then turn left and go under the motorway bridge. Turn left again at the supermarket in Quebradas and pass the school. 250m after the supermarket before the road descends round a right hand bend, you meet the levada again on the right hand side of the road, this time covered in concrete slabs.

You can now see the monumental motorway bridge ahead which spans the Socorridos valley. An extensive industrial area has been developed in the wide riverbed. The levada goes round the broad loop of a valley filled with banana trees and meets the motorway to Ribeira Brava.

The channel now bends round northwards into the Socorridos valley and gives you another view of the motorway bridge. After a little wood with eucalyptus trees and acacias you come to a place where the levada is cut into

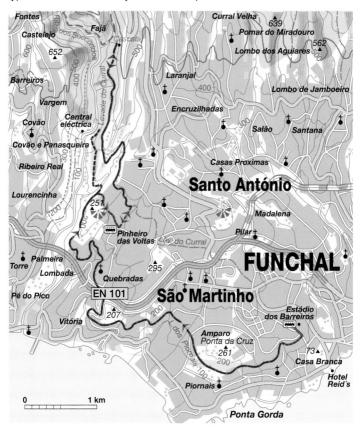

The once vertiginous section of the Levada dos Piornais is now excellently protected.

the rock and runs through short tunnels. At one time you had to go round this spectacular spot, but now there's a sturdy handrail which gives sufficient protection.

In a masterly feat of Madeiran construction the levada is taken across curving aqueducts and through several tunnels, at times only one and a half metres high (no torch necessary). After the next cut-through you reach a *set of steps*. If you do not suffer from vertigo, continue following the *Levada dos Piornais*. The **detour** leads way down into the Socorridos valley. After a bridge protected with a handrail and a short tunnel, walk for another half an hour to the power station which has been built in the valley bottom. Just after a few houses there's a red 'danger' sign and 3 minutes after that you should stop at the iron gate – the rest of the path is dangerous!

Return to the *steps* and climb up to the *Levada do Curral*. After 7 minutes turn right in front of some red iron railings onto an earth path which maintains height and turns into a road a little later on. Follow the road straight on up to the main road from **Pinheiro das Voltas**, where the bus will take you back to Funchal later.

At the Pinheiro das Voltas snack-bar go left up an alleyway (Travessa de Pinheiro das Voltas) between houses. Going straight ahead at the following fork the alleyway turns into a narrow tarmac road. Here you meet the **Levada do Curral** which you follow upstream on the left. At this point the channel is covered in slabs and leads into the lovely Ribeira do Arvoredo valley. Vine and bananas grow on both sides of the levada and smart villas are tucked in between.

Cross the streambed on a bridge and a few minutes afterwards you reach the Socorridos valley again. The *Levada do Curral* now runs on a level above the *Levada dos Piornais* across the hillside into the Socorridos valley. Precipitous points are very exposed but, in contrast to the *Levada dos Piornais* flowing 150m further below, are at first protected with wire fences.

On the other side of the valley you will soon see the green water pipes which go to the power station in the valley bottom and a picturesque hamlet tucked into the side of the valley. The levada squeezes its way through a rocky opening and there are now lengthy sections cut right into the rock. A good hour away from the snack-bar you can see the deserted houses of **Fajã**. Ahead, waterfalls thunder down into the valley. At the precipitous point where it is unprotected and becomes dangerously wet and slippery with moss, turn around and return to **Pinheiro das Voltas**.

2   To the Cabo Girão, 580m

Through the vineyards in the south

Estreito de Câmara de Lobos – Ribeira da Caixa – Cabo Girão – Cruz da Caldeira

Starting point: access from Funchal with No. 96 bus to Estreito de Câmara de Lobos as far as the Levada do Norte bus stop, about 600m after the church.
Return: from Cruz da Caldeira to Funchal with No. 4, 7 or 154 bus.
Walking time: Estreito de Câmara de Lobos – Ribeira da Caixa ¾ hr, Ribeira da Caixa – Cabo Girão 1¾ hrs, Cabo Girão – Cruz da Caldeira ¼ hr. Total time just under 2¾ hrs.
Ascent: about 50m.
Grade: leisurely levada walk without tunnels. Hardly any precipitous points.
Refreshment: Snack-bar on the Cabo Girão and in Cruz da Caldeira.
Alternative route: you can descend from the Cabo Girão along a cobbled path and a country road to the picturesque little harbour village of Câmara de Lobos. Buses go from there to Funchal or back to the starting point. There's also a taxi rank.
From the viewing platform on the cape go

past the information bureau and down the road on the right which you ascended in the last minutes up to the cliff. After a good 10 minutes the road ends in a turning circle. An old path begins here which at first zigzags downhill along an irrigation channel only a few inches wide.
Go across terraces which go right up to the precipice. The cobbled path meets a parallel-running concrete path, but you keep going straight ahead along the old path till it meets a country road after the first houses of Rancho.
The steps cross over the country road three times and the fourth time you follow the road down left to the harbour of Câmara de Lobos. Walking time about 1½ hrs.
Linking tip: combined with walk 3 you can make this into a 20km and 6 hr long levada walk. If you leave out the detour to the Cape, a torch would be helpful in the tunnel.

You will see not only walkers on the *Levada do Norte* – for many residents the irrigation channel is the only access to the house and for many children a playground. Madeira's best wines are produced on the slopes of Estreito de Câmara de Lobos, a climatically prime position. The vineyards adjoin each other on both sides of the levada like a patchwork rug and are especially beautiful in late autumn when the vine blossoms are copper-red. The spectacular coastal cliffs on the Cabo Girão are the destination for this walk.
Diagonally opposite the bus stop in **Estreito de Câmara de Lobos** at the sign 'Levada do Norte' go up four steps and stand directly on the levada. The first part of the channel is covered in slabs and runs under some picturesque pergolas. After 8 minutes you cross a track, with the channel now uncovered, and you walk along the narrow path next to the levada going upstream. A few minutes later you need to have a good head for heights at the point where the slope falls 50m steeply away to the left.

The path now gets narrower and steps lead down to the left in front of an overhanging rock. You can get around the narrowest point on a small path. The levada goes round a wide valley.

On the opposite slope you can make out the levada path cut through the greenery at the same height. Go across a metre-wide bridge over a stream. 5 minutes later you cross the **Ribeira da Caixa** on another bridge.

A precipitous section is protected with a handrail. The levada swings out of the valley and you have a view of Garachico church below. Cross the asphalt road leading to Garachico in the village of Nogueira. 25 minutes later the levada meets the wall of a water house.

Go round the house going down some steps by the rail on the left and follow the cobbled road up right until you reach the levada again. Shortly afterwards the levada path has been damaged by a landslide which has also

Above: the Canina grape grows in Estreito de Câmara de Lobos.
Right: in the villages the Levada do Norte is also a thoroughfare and is mostly covered in slabs.

caused parts of the houses above to fall into the depths. Keeping to the left you can go round this point on a little path in just a few minutes and reach the country road. Diagonally opposite the road there's a gap in the wall and steps lead down to the levada. Pass another place protected with a handrail. You can see the motorway disappearing into a tunnel below.

Quarter of an hour after the country road you are standing in front of a tunnel (if you don't want to go to the Cape, go through the 300m long tunnel and follow walk 3 to Boa Morte).

Leave the *Levada do Norte* directly in front of the tunnel and go straight ahead along the path which runs beside a 20cm wide irrigation channel. 5 minutes afterwards go across a flight of steps by a group of houses. After another 5 minutes you meet a second lot of steps which you go up to the right and in 2 minutes reach a road. This brings you in a few minutes up to the **Cabo Girão**, the highest coastal cliff in Europe. The Cape drops vertically down from the viewing platform which is usually monopolised by souvenir sellers. The view down to the well-tended terraces at the edge of the sea is spectacular.

From the Cape a road leads straight ahead to **Cruz da Caldeira**. The bus stop to Funchal is 20m left of the supermarket.

3 From Cabo Girão to Boa Morte

Westwards along the Levada do Norte

Cruz da Caldeira – Quinta Grande – Boa Morte – Barreiras

Starting point: from Funchal by car or No. 154 bus to the Cabo Girão turn-off in Cruz da Caldeira, 593m.
Return: from Barreiras by overland bus.
Walking time: Cruz da Caldeira – Quinta Grande ½ hr, Quinta Grande – Ribeira do Campanário 1 hr, Ribeira do Campanário – Boa Morte 1 hr, Boa Morte – Barreiras ¾ hr. Total time a good 3¼ hrs.
Ascent: 360m.

Grade: the levada ensures problem-free route-finding, but a head for heights would do no harm.
Long descent on a road at the end of the walk.
Refreshment: Snack-bar in Boa Morte.
Linking tip: if you do not suffer at all from vertigo you can continue following the Levada do Norte from Boa Morte (see walk 4).

With its 62km the *Levada do Norte* is the longest irrigation channel in the southwest. The section between Cabo Girão and Boa Morte runs along the upper inhabited edge of a wide valley and gives you distant views of the south side of the island as it drops down to the sea.

In **Cruz da Caldeira** go down through the village on a concrete track between the supermarket and a palm tree under which there is a well. After

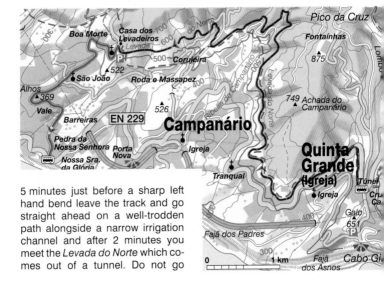

5 minutes just before a sharp left hand bend leave the track and go straight ahead on a well-trodden path alongside a narrow irrigation channel and after 2 minutes you meet the *Levada do Norte* which comes out of a tunnel. Do not go

Imposing view down from Cabo Girão to the fields at the edge of the sea.

through the tunnel, instead go left along the levada. Past some small vegetable plots you come to a stream burbling down the valley at a road bridge. Before the streambed go up to the road, follow this for 50m downhill and following the sign 'Levada do Norte' continue along the irrigation channel which at this point is covered over in slabs. You will soon see the Campanário valley below through which the motorway runs to Ribeira Brava.

Above the **Quinta Grande** the levada becomes a broad roadway for a short way. The channel crosses a small tarmac road and a concrete track and you pass the first water house. The Levada swings into a side branch of the wide Campanário valley.

At the northern-most point of the route cross the **Ribeira do Campanário** on an unprotected narrow concrete bridge. You pass a second levada house. Shortly afterwards the levada leads round a football pitch in a wide left hand bend whereby you cross over a road. The dome-shaped Pico Alto (526m) rises up ahead and soon after you can see your starting point in the northeast, the Cabo Girão, and review your whole route through the valley again.

You reach **Boa Morte** at the third levada house with a large purification plant. Go diagonally left down the roadway to the street. Past the O Pinheiro snack-bar you meet Boa Morte village crossroads. Go left at the telephone box past a bar and Café Camelo and follow the road for 45 minutes down to **Barreiras** where you meet the EN 229. The bus stop is situated right next to the 172 km-marker.

4   From Boa Morte along the Levada do Norte

Exposed levada walk for tightrope walkers

Boa Morte – Eira do Mourão – Espigão tunnel – waterfall and back

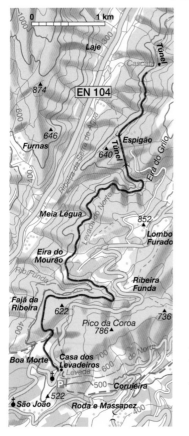

Starting point: from the EN 229 between Ribeira Brava and Campanário a road turns off sign-posted to São João and São Paulo. At both next crossroads keep going straight on uphill until you reach O Pinheiro snack-bar, 3.3 km from the EN 229.

No suitable bus service for walkers.

Walking time: Boa Morte – Eira do Mourão 1 hr, Eira do Mourão – Espigão tunnel ¾ hr, Espigão tunnel – waterfall ½ hr, return 2¼ hrs. Total time 4½ hrs.

Ascent: negligible.

Grade: a good head for heights is absolutely essential. On no account should you go any further than the point indicated – it's exceedingly dangerous! You will need a torch for the Espigão tunnel.

Refreshment: O Pinheiro snack-bar in Boa Morte.

This totally unprotected walk is reserved for levada professionals. The irrigation channel leads spectacularly over the steep and precipitous eastern edge of the Ribeira Brava basin. If you are there in September, you should include half an hour in your plans for blackberry picking.

From the O Pinheiro snack-bar in **Boa Morte** go 40m up the track to the water house which is fenced off. Follow *Levada do Norte* left upstream, cross the asphalt road after 3 minutes and you enter a mixed forest of eucalyptus, acacias and pines.

The turn-round point at the Levada do Norte – the rest of the path is dangerous!

The levada runs eastwards into the side valley of the *Ribeira Funda*. The hamlet of the same name is quite striking with its old Madeira houses and there are fig trees at the edge of the path. **Eira do Mourão** is even more picturesque. The village sits as if on display high above the Ribeira Brava basin and is only linked to the road in the valley bottom by way of a long flight of steps.

Now begins the first of the precipitous sections. The wall near to the levada path drops vertically down 200m in places. After a short 6m tunnel you pass a usually muddy overflow and rivulets trickle onto the path from the hillside covered in metre-long grasses. Now and then the levada runs under overhanging rocks.

You reach the **Espigão tunnel**. After 8 minutes you have walked 'beneath' Espigão hamlet, so to speak, which lies on the mountain ridge high above the almost one kilometre long tunnel. Immediately after the tunnel you come to some more precipitous places which require your undivided attention, despite the marvellous views of Serra de Água and the Encumeada pass.

25 Minutes after the tunnel exit the levada goes round a wide right hand bend, right across the middle of a vertical rock face. Small **waterfalls** tumble down into the valley and you can see the entrance to another tunnel further on. At this point you break off from this increasingly dangerous walk and return the same way.

5 Fontes

Round walk with splendid views on comfortable earth tracks

Fontes – Chão dos Terreiros – Trompica forestry house – Fontes

Starting point: from the EN 229 between Ribeira Brava and Campanário a road turns off sign-posted to São João and São Paulo. Keep going straight uphill at both crossroads in the direction of São Paulo. Shortly after the O Pinheiro snack-bar cross over the Levada do Norte and pass a cement factory. Drive below the church of São Paulo in the direction of Fontes which you will reach in 9km from the EN 229. You can park in the small village square in front of Bar Fontes.

Walking time: Fontes – Chão dos Terreiros 1¼ hrs, Chão dos Terreiros – Trompica forestry house ¾ hr, forestry house – Fontes ½ hr. Total time 2½ hrs.

Ascent: 450m, the same in descent.

Grade: problem-free walk with a long ascent on a broad and sometimes stony unpaved earth track.

Refreshment: Bar Fontes at the start of the walk.

The high mountain trail round Fontes is one of the few round walks on Madeira and also one with excellent views. Fontes seems poor in spite of some new houses and gives you the impression of having missed out on all contact with modern Madeira.

At the village square in **Fontes** near the red post box at the bar, a concrete path leads steeply uphill with a few thatched Madeira cottages on either side. At the upper edge of the village the concrete path turns into a broad earth track. Sweet chestnut and eucalyptus trees line the path on the one-hour climb to a pass from where there's a beautiful view of the Ribeira Brava valley and the Encumeada pass.

The earth track bends round to the east. The Pico da Cruz (1311m) on your left seems almost near enough to reach out and touch from here and way below you can see São Paulo church. At the fork 10 minutes later maintaining height take the left track and climb over a pasture fence. 5 minutes after another fence the path branches off left. The now difficult-to-find grassy path ends shortly in a notch.

From there keep to the right and climb up a distinct path in a good 5 minutes to the trig point on **Chão dos Terreiros** (1436m). The viewing summit affords not only views of Curral das Freiras and the central massif, but you can

Reed-thatched Madeira cottages in Fontes.

also make out Funchal harbour in the southeast. From the summit go back to the fork and turn off here sharp left downhill. After several cattle gates you come to **Trompica forestry house** and after 20 minutes you meet the new road to Campanário where you turn right and go back up to **Fontes** village square in 15 minutes.

6 Tabua valley

Entertaining walk through the beautiful Ribeira da Tabua valley

Ribeira Brava – Sítio da Ribeira da Tabua – Candelária – Ribeira Brava

Starting point: by car or bus to Ribeira Brava.

Walking time: Ribeira Brava – Levada Nova 1 hr, Levada Nova – Sítio da Ribeira da Tabua 1 hr, Sítio da Ribeira da Tabua – Candelária 1 hr, Candelária – Ribeira Brava 1 hr. Total time 4 hrs.

Ascent: 400m, the same in descent.

Grade: ascent to the levada requires fitness and the path alongside the levada requires a good head for heights. A torch is helpful in the 50m long tunnel. Take your swimwear!

Refreshment: Água Mar beach restaurant in Ribeira Brava with good fish dishes.

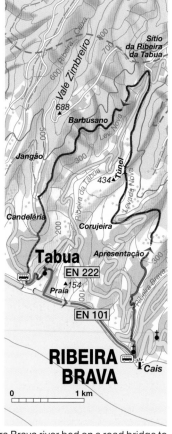

This walk acquaints you with the very attractive Ribeira da Tabua valley. A continuous rural exodus has caused so many of the terraces to lie fallow and the hamlet of Barbusano is as good as deserted. And yet bananas, vine, sweet potatoes and sugar cane are still cultivated. This is a good walk to test your lack of vertigo.

From the bus stop in **Ribeira Brava**, opposite the *tourist information* in an old fortified tower, go westwards along the coast road for 100m. Before the river bridge turn right into the road to São Vicente/Funchal. Leave this again after 100m by crossing the broad Ribeira Brava river bed on a road bridge to the left side. From the bridge you can already see the steep *flight of steps* going high up.

The Levada Nova is reached up a steep flight of steps.

After 6 minutes the steps meet the road again. By following this uphill you soon reach the beautifully paved river-stone path again. The flight of steps goes through a village and becomes a very steep roadway. At the first well keep straight ahead and take the right hand concrete path at the fork.

At the third well above a reed-covered Madeira house leave the concrete path and go up some wide steps on the right. After 15 minutes you pass a round water tank. In 50m you come past a junk shop after which you turn left to reach the **Levada Nova**.

Cherry blossom in the Tabua valley.

The ascent is now behind you. The levada doesn't look much – it is only 30cm wide – and the path which you follow for the next 2 hours upstream is not much wider. After only 4 minutes the levada goes under a road. It flows a few metres next to the road on the other side and then continues to the right above the road. A good 10 minutes further on the channel disappears under the road again. Continue along the road to the right for 50m until some steps cross over. Go down these to the left to meet the levada again.

Now begins the first of the precipitous places and you should not allow yourself to be distracted by the view of the Ribeira da Tabua valley – the path is actually quite easy but demands your full attention.

After crossing a road you walk through a 50m tunnel. At the end of the valley the levada just reaches the hamlet of **Sítio da Ribeira da Tabua**. Cross over the road coming from the valley bottom and shortly afterwards you meet the first of three inflows of the Ribeira da Tabua where you have to wade through a ford.

You cross the second arm of the river at the northern-most point of the route on an iron bridge. Now the levada runs on the west side of the valley down to the sea again. The ford over the third inflow can be wet and slippery after periods of bad weather.

7 minutes after the ford a mountain-spur below some 2m high rocks provides a picnic spot with good views.

The levada ends at the entrance to **Candelária** and you follow a concrete roadway down past some sugar cane fields. The path meets an asphalt road onto which you turn left only to leave it again immediately right, below the sports field, along a concrete roadway running southwards. This now goes very steeply down to the tarmac road which you descend for 250m. Go right again and continue your descent on a concrete path.

You meet the main road in the bottom of the valley. Turn right and in 5 minutes you come to the sea. The very busy main road brings you in 20 minutes back to **Ribeira Brava** – as long as you don't stop off at the beach or the Água Mar fish restaurant on the way.

Depending on the level of the water you can get wet feet at the ford.

7 Lombada da Ponta do Sol

Vertiginous round walk through the Ribeira da Ponta do Sol valley

Solar dos Esmeraldos – Levada Nova – Levada do Moinho – Solar dos Esmeraldos

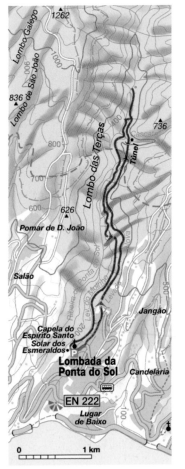

Starting point: coming from Funchal drive along the coast road as far as the entrance to the village of Ponta do Sol and 200m before the big roundabout turn up left. When you meet the EN 222 keep right as far as Lombada da Ponta do Sol. Above the village you can already see the striking manor house Solar dos Esmeraldos painted in traditional pink and a chapel nearby to which there's a road leading up on the left. You can park between the manor house and the chapel.

Walking time: Solar dos Esmeraldos – Levada Nova ¼ hr, Levada Nova – Levada Nova source 1 hr, source – Levada do Moinho 10 min, Levada do Moinho – Solar dos Esmeraldos 1½ hrs. Total time 3 hrs.

Ascent: 80 m.

Grade: a good head for heights is absolutely essential for both levadas, precipitous places are not protected. While it's an easy walk along the little wall of the Levada Nova, the path next to the Levada do Moinho is very overgrown and has broken away in places. Long trousers are recommended as a protection against ticks. You will need a torch for the tunnel and rainwear for the waterfall.

Refreshment: no facilities on the way.

Lombada da Ponta do Sol lies in a picturesque location on a mountain ridge running inland from the sea. Starting point for this beautiful levada walk is the big Solar dos Esmeraldos manor house in which the Flemish sugar baron, Jean

Ponta da Sol on the south coast is one of the sunniest corners of the island – from here you can see the sunrise as well as the sunset.

d'Esmenaut (Portuguese João Esmeraldo), used to reside 500 years ago. The Flemish man is supposed to have been a good friend of Christopher Columbus. His wealth came from the extensive estates round the village where Moorish slaves tended the sugar cane. In the Espíritu Santo chapel next to the estate is to be found the tomb of Esmeraldo and the former manor house now houses the village school.

After visiting the baroque chapel and the old sugar mill go from the **Solar dos Esmeraldos** 200m back to the road which you came on and follow this straight up ahead. At the crossroads 100m further on (sign 3.5 tons) turn left onto a small road going up steeply,after 300m at a well cross over a road and shortly afterwards you come to a fork at another well. Right by the fork there are some metre-wide steps leading up to the **Levada Nova**.

Follow the channel upstream through sugar cane fields and after 4 minutes cross over a road. In summer blue Lilies of the Nyle line the path and in winter, the funnel-shaped white Calla Lilies, while the Ribeira da Ponta do Sol burbles below.

You are walking all the way along the small 40cm wide wall of the levada, precipitous in places, which runs deeper and deeper inland on the right valley hillside. One section of the path covered in climbing ivy is especially pretty, although very precipitous. Down to the sea you have a beautiful view of the chapel at the start of the walk.

After three quarters of an hour on the levada you reach a 200m long *tunnel*. You can see the other end and by crouching down a little, however quite easily and with dry feet, you can walk through to daylight at the other end. Now it gets damp. A *waterfall* ahead has worn a broad groove into the rock and thunders down onto the levada wall in spectacular fashion – you can't escape a shower in winter.

The levada has now caught up with the stony river bed. On the left pass a path running into the valley and shortly afterwards a grating with a small pool from which a subsidiary levada flows down into the valley. Eventually you reach the **Levada Nova spring** where the rocks in the river bed provide idyllic picnic spots.

From the spring go back along the levada and 3 minutes after the grating descend the inconspicuous, extremely steep path in 2 minutes to the **Levada do Moinho** which runs about 10m parallel above the river bed. A concrete slab laid across the levada marks the point of descent. The grassy path along the 'mill levada' whose water previously drove the sugar mill of the Solar dos Esmeraldos is not in use any more and is very overgrown. Increasingly you need to force your way through ferns and blackberry bushes and scramble over trees which have fallen right across the levada. You reach the trickiest point about 10 minutes after the second cattle gate. You can walk round the channel which is overgrown with big-leaved Taro Root on a wet and slippery small path to the right.

Soon the chapel comes into view again. But, after the first vegetable plots which have been dug into the hillside, you need to give your full attention to the occasionally precipitous path until the levada eventually brings you back again round behind the chapel to the **Solar dos Esmeraldos**.

A walk along the Levada Nova in the Ribeira Ponta do Sol valley presupposes a lack of vertigo.

8 From Monte to Camacha

On the Lily of the Nyle levada into the village of basket weavers

Monte – Palheiro Ferreiro – Ribeirinha – Camacha

Starting point: from Funchal with No. 20 or 21 local bus as far as Monte terminus, 590m.

Return: from Camacha to Funchal with No. 29 bus.

Walking time: Monte – Curral dos Romeiros ¾ hr, Curral dos Romeiros – Quinta do Pomar ¾ hr, Quinta do Pomar – Palheiro Ferreiro 1 hr, Palheiro Ferreiro – Ribeirinha 1 hr, Ribeirinha – Camacha 1 hr. Total time just under 4½ hrs.

Ascent: 100m descent, 300m ascent.

Grade: apart from leisurely ascents and descents at the start an easy levada walk as far as Palheiro Ferreiro. But after Palheiro Ferreiro there's a really unpleasant tunnel to get through for which each person needs a torch. Absolute sure-footedness is essential. Some route-

finding ability is necessary as you go round Ribeirinha.

Refreshment: two tea houses on the way, and Café Relógio in Camacha.

Alternative route 1: if you want to avoid the unpleasant tunnel you can break the walk at Palheiro Ferreiro and take the bus back to Funchal.

Alternative route 2: at the Quinta do Pomar you can ascend the little road up left in a good 20 minutes to the Levada da Serra and follow this right, through the Vale Paraiso as far as Camacha (walk 9 backwards). By going this way you can also avoid the tunnel.

Linking tip: those walkers who are fit can continue from Camacha to the Largo do Miranda (walk 9) and take a bus from there back to Funchal.

Starting point of the walk is Monte which, with the pilgrimage church, the starting point of the carros de cesto (wicker basket tobbogan) and an exotic botanical garden, has three of the top tourist attractions on Madeira. The crowds at the start are correspondingly big but after only a few minutes you leave behind the hustle and bustle and the beautiful walk begins.

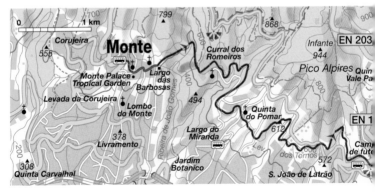

From the main square in **Monte** leave the Café do Parque on the left hand side and turn right into the Caminho dos Babosos. The beautiful path, surfaced in river gravel, brings you in just under 200m to the starting place for the carros de cesto (wicker basket toboggans). Continuing straight ahead glance upwards to the famous *pilgrimage church Nossa Senhora do Monte* and shortly afterwards go past the entrance to the *Monte Palace Tropical Garden*.

After a few minutes you come to the pretty circular Largo das Babosas square with a chapel. From the parapet there's a fine view into the valley of the Ribeira de João Gomes. Descend from the square along the paved Caminho Padre Eugenio Borgonovo. Take no notice of a left turn-off after 7 minutes.

A bridge goes over the Ribeira de João Gomes and zigzags steeply up to the **Curral dos Romeiros**. Stay on the main path and go through the delightfully situated village on the hillside. At the end of the village you will see a tarmac road below. Don't go down to this, instead go left up some steps. One minute later you come to the *Levada dos Tornos*. If you are there during the main flowering time between May and September you will be struck by the Lilies of the Nyle planted along the channel.

At the **Quinta do Pomar** estate the levada disappears under a road. Cross over the road and go through a red iron gate (if it's shut, go left 100m up the road and go round the estate). After the chapel of the Quinta house you meet the levada again.

Further along you cross over two roads and pass the *Hortensia Gardens Tea House*. After crossing another road the *Jasmin Tea House* is an inviting place to stop for tea and a vegetable soup. Just under 20 minutes after the tea house you reach the EN 102 (you could break the walk here by following the road down to the next bus stop or going on to Palheiro Gardens).

The levada path continues at the other side of the road. The channel runs below the **Palheiro Ferreiro** football pitch and for a short way disappears, at which point you continue straight ahead on the path until the levada pops up again afterwards.

Cross another road and a good 10 minutes later you are standing in front of a tunnel. You can see the end of the tunnel, but it takes 12 minutes to reach it. The path in the tunnel is sometimes only 30cm wide and the narrowest place is roughly in the middle. It's also quite damp in places and so low that you have to bend down to get through.

It's an advantage not to have too large a rucksack with you in case it bangs against the wall and throws you off balance. So switch on your torch and off you go!

In **Ribeirinha** the levada runs for a short way parallel to the village road. After it's covered for a second time with slabs climb up the steps left to the road and follow this to the right (after a few minutes a landslide along the levada stops you going any further). The village road goes uphill through an

The carros de cesto (wicker basket tobbogan) in Monte –
once a local form of transport, today a tourist attraction.

The pilgrimage church in Monte.

area of new housing and in just under 10 minutes a road leads in from above left. Go straight on at the next crossroads, pass the No. 114 bus stop on the left and meet the main road Caniço – Camacha. Follow this down left for 100m and then turn off right.

Keep straight ahead at the small crossroads 100m later. The little road leads down into a small valley. Cross a stream over a bridge and 50m further up a sign points right to the *Levada dos Tornos*. The path forks after 25m. Go straight ahead and at the next fork take the right hand path and eventually you will reach the levada again.

Follow the channel left downstream, cross over two roads and come to a house with a striking date palm in front. A little later the levada runs into a long tunnel (it's possible here to continue along walk 15).

In front of the tunnel descend a few steps to a cobbled path which you follow steeply uphill to *Salgados*. At the Eira Salgada bar the path meets the asphalt village road to **Camacha** which brings you up steeply to the village square. The craft centre with *Café Relógio* is in the building with the clock tower. The busses leave from the other end of the square.

9 From Camacha to Largo do Miranda

Through 'paradise valley' to the botanical garden

Camacha – Vale Paraiso – Quinta do Pomar – Largo do Miranda – botanical garden

Starting point: from Funchal with No. 29 bus to Camacha, 700 m.
Return: from the Largo do Miranda (480m) to Funchal with No. 30 local bus.
Walking time: Camacha – Achadinha ½ hr, Achadinha – Quinta do Pomar 2 hrs, Quinta do Pomar – Largo do Miranda ¼ hr, Largo do Miranda – botanical garden ¼ hr. Total time 3 hrs.

Ascent: just under 50m and about 250m in descent.
Grade: short climb at the beginning and steep descent at the end, otherwise an easy walk and for the most part a shady and broad levada path.
Refreshment: Moisés snack-bar in Achadinha.

A King Protea (Cape Artichoke-Flower) in the botanical garden.

With its nearness to Funchal and because of the leisurely path, the walk along the *Levada da Serra* is one of the most popular walks on the island. The walk is still attractive even if sometimes there is no water left in the irrigation channel. The diverse flora at the edge of the path is enough to convince you from a botanical point of view. And if that's not enough you can still visit Funchal's botanical garden at the end of the walk. An easy levada walk to get you going.

From the bus stop in the large village square Largo da Achada in **Camacha** go back a few steps and follow the road uphill to Santo António da Serra. Go past the post office and the church and after 200m turn left into a narrow little road (sign 'Levada da Serra da Faial'). At a crossroads you come to the levada hidden under concrete slabs and you turn left at the sign 'Levada da Serra/Choupana'. Ancient tree ferns are growing in the front gardens of the cottages. You soon leave the last houses behind to walk through a luxuriant green valley.

In **Achadinha** the levada gets lost for a short way. At the *Moisés snack-bar* you come to a crossroads and continue straight ahead out of the village on the asphalt road. At a bus stop after 150m steps lead up right to the levada again.

The path now goes through jungle-like vegetation. You walk round a wide bend through the **Vale Paraiso**. An hour after Achadinha cross the EN 203.

The levada now runs through a dense wood which is intermingled with the remains of laurel trees. The tree trunks are covered in ivy right up the top and long beardmoss hangs down from the branches.

The channel flows more and more sparsely until eventually there's no more water left. In places the levada is totally submerged, but the path is well-kept. Keep right at the fork shortly after the ruins of a house and 10 minutes afterwards the levada meets a cobbled path and stops unexpectedly. Descend steeply down the cobbled track, cross over a road and continue down a the small tarmac road (Caminho da Meio). After passing the entrance to the Campo do Pomar (football stadium) you soon reach the first houses of **Choupana**.

Continue going downhill at a fork and after 2 minutes cross over the *Levada dos Tornos* (walk 8) at the **Quinta do Pomar**. Pass a red iron gate on the left and a little later the entrance to the Quinta and 10 minutes after that leave the road on a cobbled path descending straight ahead. The sea of houses and the harbour of Funchal come into view below.

The cobbled path meets an asphalt road in **Largo do Miranda**. The bus stop is just on the right in front of the *Restaurant Miranda*. If you like you can go 15 minutes down the road to the **botanical garden** and take a bus from there.

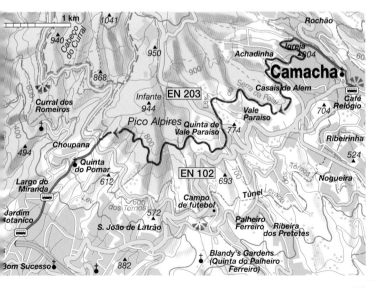

The east and Ribeiro Frio

Caniço has become a popular holiday resort in the last two decades. The suburb of *Caniço de Baixo* along the steep coast guarantees relaxing holidays, however without an actual centre there is not the atmosphere you expect from a resort. Many visitors are familiar with the pebbly beach of Reis Magos as well as the two idyllic swimming places Lido Galomar and Lido Rocamar where, after a day's walking, you can have a swim in the sea.

On the nearby *Ponta do Garajau* a statue of Christ can be seen from a long way off. The coastal area around the cliff is designated as an underwater nature reserve in which no fishing is allowed. The area is especially popular with divers and there are several diving schools.

The explorer João Gonçalves Zarco landed in the pretty bay of **Machico** in 1419 and took possession of the then uninhabited island for Portugal. From the small harbour of today's third largest town on Madeira tuna fishing is a thriving business and boat trips are organised to the Peninsula São Lourenço and onto the Desertas bird islands. You can go on walks along the *Levada do Caniçal* into the green hinterland characterised by a range of gentle hills.

A lift goes down the steep coast to the sea-water pool in Caniço de Baixo.

Typical of Madeira – fertile terraced countryside at Cruzinhas.

At the foot of Pico do Facho a 750m long tunnel runs through the mountain ridge between Machico and **Caniçal**. The flat belt of land round the former whaling village is Madeira's driest region. The trade winds find no obstacle here, particularly over the Ponta de São Lourenço promontory which pushes right out into the sea, and now and again clouds sweep gustily across the barren rocky landscape. Quite unassuming prickly pears and euphorbia bushes thrive well in the barren scenery dominated by soft ochre-tones.

Until 1981 when Portugal recognised the Washington agreement for the protection of species the sperm whales were hunted from Caniçal. In four decades almost 6000 of the up to 20m long mammals were killed. Their fat was coveted in the cosmetic industry. The meat and bones were used to make cattle feed and fertilizer in a factory.

At a height of 850m and only a dozen kilometres inland from the dry east coast lies one of the wet areas of the island with the **Ribeiro Frio**. In the luxuriant green region around the 'cold river' there are extensive laurel forests with quite a few plants which only grow in Madeira. The state-run trout farm is also worth a visit. In the pools fed by mountain water 80.000 fish are bred annually. In the small botanical garden at the forestry house you can marvel at the spring-blossoming camelia trees. Ribeiro Frio is the starting point for two of the most popular levada walks on Madeira.

10 Through the Porto Novo valley

Along the quiet Levada do Caniço to Assumada

Camacha – Salgados – Assumada

Starting point/return: from Funchal with No. 29 bus to Camacha, 700m. Return from Assumada (230m) with one of the busses along the coast road.

It's a good idea for car drivers to park in Assumada and get a taxi to Camacha.

Walking time: Camacha – Salgados 20 min, Salgados – Assumada 1½ hrs. Total time 1 hr 50 min.

Descent: 470m.

Grade: steep descent on old cobbled path (slippery when wet), then a leisurely levada walk with a few precipitous sections, but without making you feel dizzy.

Refreshment: small bar in Salgados and restaurants in Assumada.

From the basket weaving village of Camacha an old link path goes down into the almost deserted hamlet of Salgados and an idyllic levada path continues through the secluded Porto Novo valley. Up to only a few decades ago ox-pulled carts used to travel the well-preserved cobbled path. A worthwhile walk in spite of its brevity.

From the bus stop in the village square in **Camacha** go towards the *Café Relógio* at the clock tower. Go past a chapel and the health centre (Centro Saúde) and leave the square to the right along a small road sign-posted 'Assomada/Caniço' amongst other places. The road descends steeply and after 10 minutes you go past *Eira Salgada bar* and a sign points right to the *Levada dos Tornos* (walk 15). However you carry straight on down towards the big school building. Just before it turn left onto a path which is tarmac at first and cobbled a little later, and descends steeply. Walk through the picturesque hamlet of **Salgados** nestling into the hillside of the Porto Novo valley. The steps become more narrow, uneven and even steeper until they eventually meet at the lower edge of the village the *Levada do Caniço* which you follow downstream. Along the path there are willows which provide the raw material for the popular basket weaving in the surrounding villages. Soon the whole of the Porto Novo valley lies at your feet and you can see the silhouette of the Ilhas Desertas ahead.

Descent to the hamlet of Salgados on 'ox-foot cobbles'.

Now walk through a 15m long tunnel where there is no need for a torch. Before the tunnel you can go along a path to a picnic spot with a beautiful view of the exit to the valley and the bridge for the coast road as it spans the valley.

Shortly before the first houses of Assumada there's a concrete path along the levada and you pass a round water tank on the left. In front of the first house on the path you leave the levada at a water purification plant and turn left onto a concrete path which descends to the already visible road.

Down this to the left after a good 15 minutes you come to **Assumada** church. The bus stop is 50m east of the church, directly on the EN 204.

11 Over Pico do Facho to Caniçal

On the whalers' path along the coast

Caniçal tunnel – Pico do Facho – Caniçal

Starting point/return: from Funchal by car or No. 113 bus to Pico do Facho stop right in front of the Caniçal tunnel, 220m. Return from Caniçal with No. 113 bus as well. Park your car in front of the tunnel and return to the car by bus.
Walking time: Caniçal tunnel – Pico do Facho ½ hr, Pico do Facho – Caniçal tunnel 1½ hrs. Total time 2 hrs.

Ascent: 100m, and 320m in descent.
Grade: stony coastal path without any shade; helpful red waymarkings on the sometimes overgrown path. At times it can be quite windy.
Refreshment: several snack-bars in Caniçal round the village square and the Panoramico fish restaurant.

Madeira reveals its dry side on the old whalers' path. Along the east coast unassuming Prickly pears provide green dots in the otherwise ochre-coloured landscape. In Caniçal a small whale museum (Museu da Baleia) documents the eventful history of whalers who hunted sperm whales until the 80s.

In front of the **Caniçal tunnel** turn onto the road sign-posted 'Pico do Facho'. After a quarter of an hour an earth track turns off in front of an electricity pylon. But first you go up to **Pico do Facho** (322m). The 'torch mountain' was previously a pirates' look-out post. As soon as a boat was sighted

Machico bay seen from Pico do Facho.

a beacon was lit in order to mobilize defences. You have a wonderful view of Machico bay from the picnic spot below the pylons.

Back at the electricity pylon at the dug-out you follow the earth track right which narrows to a small path after 150m. First you can enjoy the magnificent panorama of the São Lourenço peninsula jutting far out to sea. The path forks after a few metres and you keep to the right – a faded red waymarking guides you over the path which is exposed in short sections.

The stony path leads down into a valley then climbs up towards an electricity pylon. From the rocky ridge at the pylon you can look down to your destination, Caniçal harbour.

A few minutes below the ridge the path heads towards an arched bridge. At the bridge you meet a stony roadway which you follow uphill. You come to an area fenced off with wire netting, go right along the path beside the fence and come to a roadway again at the seaward side. Further along the fence you approach a palm grove. The tarmac road at the sea brings you straight to **Caniçal** harbour. At the roundabout in front of the petrol station go up left to the whale museum and above that to the church, taxi rank and bus stop.

12 São Lourenço peninsula

Spectacular rocky coast in the furthest eastern corner of the island

Baía da Abra – Casa do Sardinha and back

Starting point: as you leave Caniçal by car follow the signs to 'Prainha/Baía d'Abra' and drive for about 5km, past the post office and the free trade harbour (Zona Franca), until the road ends at a car park. In summer buses go as far as Prainha.

Walking time: Baía da Abra – Casa do Sardinha 1 hr, Casa da Sardinha – mountain with spectacular views ½ hr, return 1¼ hrs. Total time 2½ hrs.

Ascent: 100m.

Grade: sure-footedness and a good head for heights are essential on this demanding walk on stony mule paths. According to the Rother grading this walk lies in the dark red to black category. Take your swimwear!

Refreshment: mobile kiosque at the car park (only in the season) and the sophisticated Quinta do Lorde restaurant on the approach road.

As you fly into Madeira over the peninsula, your impressions certainly do not correspond to the cliché of the evergreen island of flowers. It's true that after rainy winters the finger-like peninsula pointing out into the sea is covered in a greenish down, but in summer it appears totally arid except for the simple Hottentot figs. The wildly romantic coast makes the walk very popular – a rocky and contrasting alternative to the evergreen levada paths.

From the car park above **Baía da Abra** at the end of the road descend an earth track past two rocky boulders into a small valley and after 150m keep to the right. If you look across the peninsula you can see a circular rock arch over the water and above this a conspicuous mountain – this is your destination. There's a fork in the path 15 minutes from the car park. Going left you come quickly to a spectacular viewpoint of the strangely shaped coast with a 30m high rock tower like a cathedral rising up out of the water (see photo on p. 2).

Back at the fork you now begin a short steep ascent. Climb up steps over a rocky ridge without any paths past waymarkings and cairns to another viewpoint, again with imposing views of a steep rock face riven by stone gullies. The path goes round Abra bay in a wide arc on the south side of the peninsula.

At the same height as the round fish farm floating in the sea there's now a tricky section of the path, but it's protected with wire cables. The path runs over a land bridge at the narrowest point of the peninsula. On both sides the rock drops down vertically 100m. You come to the **Casa do Sardinho** which is surrounded by date palms and stands out like an oasis from the rust to curry-yellow coloured landscape. Leave the house on the right hand side and above it start the straight-lined ascent to the mountain-top with wonderful views (146m). In spite of the relatively low altitude there's an impressive panorama from the summit over to the lighthouse on the Ilhéu do Farol, which looks as if it's just hanging there, and to the neighbouring island of Porto Santo.

On the return you should stop for a swim. At the viewpoint a quarter of an hour away from the car park there's a well-trodden path which brings you in a few minutes down to the stony beach in Baía da Abra. If you prefer a sandy beach you should head for Prainha. Of the few beaches where swimming is possible on Madeira, it is the best.

The land bridge, just a few metres wide, marks the narrowest point of Sâo Lourenço.

13 From Maroços to the Caniçal tunnel

Gentle stroll along the Levada do Caniçal

Maroços – Ribeira Grande – Ribeira Seca – Caniçal tunnel

Starting point: from Funchal by car or No. 156 bus to Maroços, 200m.
Return: to Funchal from the Caniçal tunnel (220m) with No. 113 bus. You must change in Machico to return to Maroços.
Walking time: Maroços – Ribeira Grande 1 hr, Ribeira Grande -Ribeira Seca 1½ hrs, Ribeira Seca – Caniçal tunnel ¾ hr. Total time 3½ hrs.

Ascent: negligible.
Grade: easy 12km long levada walk without any vertiginous sections.
Refreshment: O Tunel restaurant on the EN 190, 250m down from the tunnel.
Linking tip: you can combine this walk with walk 11 to Caniçal.
There's a coastal path via Boca do Risco to Porto da Cruz (walk 14).

The *Levada do Caniçal* is the only irrigation channel in the dry northeast of Madeira. For the building of the levada in 1949 they drilled a 750m long tunnel through the mountain ridge at the foot of Pico do Facho which was widened for cars some years later. The appeal of the walk lies in the alternating densely cultivated land and deep and quiet ravine-like valleys with unspoiled nature. The side valleys of the Ribeira de Machico are particularly lovely in spring when the acacia is flowering.

From the bus stop in **Maroços** follow the road by the conspicuously large school building with the red window frames for one kilometre uphill as far as the *Bar Fonte Vermelha* (you can park your car here). 10m before the bar there's a sharp right hand turn-off onto a concrete path. The *Levada do Caniçal* next to it is covered with slabs at first and protected with a handrail.

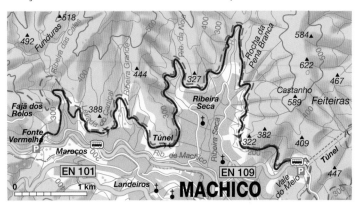

Damp natural habitat in the Ribeira das Cales valley.

After you have passed the last houses of Maroços the channel runs deep into the valley of the Ribeira das Cales which you cross over on a bridge. Go back a short way into the residential zone until the levada swings round into the valley of the **Ribeira Grande**. At the deepest part of the valley a signpost points you the remaining 9km towards the Caniçal tunnel. You don't need a torch to walk through the 25m long tunnel. After the tunnel you have a beautiful view of the roofs of Machico and the transmitters on Pico do Facho, and you can also see the Desertas islands.

The Ribeira da Noia and Ribeira Seca valleys follow the Ribeira Grande valley. You will soon see the curved saddle of the Boca do Risco, a pass which separates the Ribeira Seca valley from the north coast.

Just after the wash place in front of the first house of **Ribeira Seca**, a path coming up from the valley crosses the levada which leads up to *Boca do Risco* (walk 14). Continue following the levada straight ahaid and in 45 minutes you reach the EN 109 at the **Caniçal tunnel**. You can flag down the bus in front of the wash house.

14 From the Caniçal tunnel to Porto da Cruz

Adventurous coastal path over the 'dangerous gap'

Caniçal tunnel – Boca do Risco – Larano – Porto da Cruz

Starting point/return: from Funchal by car or No. 113 bus to the western side of the Caniçal tunnel (bus stop Pico do Facho), 220m.

Return from Porto da Cruz via Machico to Funchal with No. 53 bus.

If you have to return to your car, turn round at the Espigão Amarelo and you will have then experienced the most impressive section of the walk.

Walking time: Caniçal tunnel – Boca do Risco 80 min, Boca do Risco – Espigão Amarelo 50 min, Espigão Amarelo – Larano 50 min, Larano – Porto da Cruz 50 min. Total time just under 4 hrs.

Ascent: just under 200m, descent 400m.

Grade: a problem-free levada walk as far as Boca do Risco. Total sure-footedness and a good head for heights is needed for the rest of the walk along the coastal path. Do not attempt in stormy weather or when wet. Landslides can make the path impassable. Take your swimwear with you for the sea-water pool at Porto da Cruz.

Refreshment: no facilities on the way. Penha d'Ave restaurant in Porto da Cruz.

Along the coastal path over the sea-washed north coast.

The north coast at Porto da Cruz.

Hiking paths along the coast of Madeira are in short supply as the land drops away too abruptly into the sea. For this reason they are even more exciting when they do exist.

The coastal path from Machico and Porto da Cruz was for centuries the shortest link route between the two places. So-called Borracheiros brought the young wine in goatskins over the Boca do Risco ('dangerous notch') on foot. The reasonably well-maintained path high above the crashing waves of the sea has lost none of its wildness today.

From the bus stop directly in front of the **Caniçal tunnel** cross the road to the *Levada do Caniçal* at the small water house. Follow the channel upstream through a small acacia wood into the Ribeira Seca valley.

After three quarters of an hour of leisurely walking along a comfortable path next to the levada you need to be careful: 50m after a *line of pylons carrying electric power* up from the valley a footpath crosses the levada diagonally. Leave the channel here and go up the path sharply to the right. Soon you will be able to see the curved saddle of Boca do Risco above. At the fork take the right hand path, branch off left 13 minutes later and walk round some private property.

After a half-hour ascent you reach **Boca do Risco**. There's usually a stiff breeze at the top of the pass, but the view of the bizarrely structured north coast more than compensates for it.

From the pass follow the broad coastal path down in a westerly direction first of all. Tree heathers line the edge of the path so that the precipitous hillside appears harmless. With butterflies in your stomach you soon spot the path cut into the almost vertical cliff.

Walk through a goat gate and a few minutes later you come to the trickiest part of the path where there are yawning chasms of almost 400m. A wire cable protects one section of broken path and after rainfall a rivulet of water provides you with a shower.

The subsequent wobbly wooden fences are more a psychological than a real support.

A knee-high trig point marks the rock projection of Espigão Amarelo and from here you can see the jagged silhouette of the Ponta de São Lourenço in the east. Shortly afterwards you step through another gate and you now have a glorious view of Eagle Rock ahead and Porto da Cruz.

The most difficult sections are now over. Cross an idyllically overgrown stream bed on sometimes slippery rocks and after two other streams

The Lily of the Nyle is ever-present on Madeira.

64

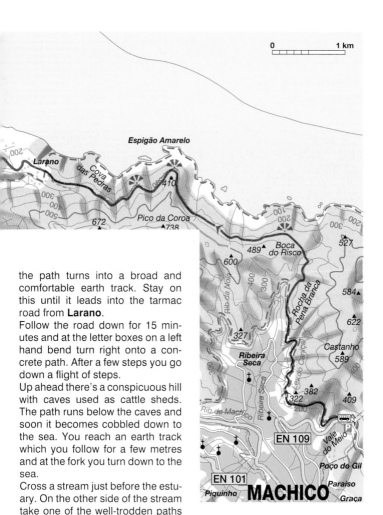

the path turns into a broad and comfortable earth track. Stay on this until it leads into the tarmac road from **Larano**.

Follow the road down for 15 minutes and at the letter boxes on a left hand bend turn right onto a concrete path. After a few steps you go down a flight of steps.

Up ahead there's a conspicuous hill with caves used as cattle sheds. The path runs below the caves and soon it becomes cobbled down to the sea. You reach an earth track which you follow for a few metres and at the fork you turn down to the sea.

Cross a stream just before the estuary. On the other side of the stream take one of the well-trodden paths which lead to a flight of steps to bring you up to the road.

Going right you will reach the Porto da Cruz church after 10 minutes. Taxis wait in the village square and the bus stop is a short way above before the Centro de Saúde on the main street.

15 From Camacha to Sítio das Quatro Estradas

On the Passion Flower path along the Levada dos Tornos

Camacha – Lombo Grande – Ribeira dos Vinháticos – Sítio das Quatro Estradas

Trailing Passion Flower.

Starting point: from Funchal by car or No. 29 bus to Camacha, 700m.
Return: from Sítio das Quatro Estradas (750m) to Camacha or Funchal with No. 77 bus.
Walking time: Camacha – Lombo Grande 1½ hrs, Lombo Grande – Ribeira dos Vinháticos 1 hr, Ribeira dos Vinháticos – end of the Levada dos Tornos 1½ hrs, end of levada – Sítio das Quatro Estradas

½ hr. Total time a good 4½ hrs.
Descent: 100m, 150m in ascent.
Grade: long levada walk, only suitable for those who do not suffer from vertigo. In winter the paths can be slippery in places with draining rivulets and small waterfalls as well as wet leaves. A torch is needed for the tunnels.
Refreshment: no facilities on the way except for the small bar in Salgados.

With its length of over 100km the *Levada dos Tornos*, built 35 years ago, is one of the most important aqueducts on the island. 16km of it is channelled through tunnels. The levada begins above Boaventura and runs across the whole island.

Keen walkers will have already become acquainted with it in walk 8. Today's route takes you to the end of the *Levada dos Tornos*. Along the way you can marvel at the terraced fields and trailing maracujas. Distant views of the east coast open up again and again.

From the bus stop in **Camacha** village square go towards the *Café Relógio* at the clock tower. Go past a chapel and the health centre (Centro de Saúde) and leave the square along a small road on the right which is sign-posted 'Levada dos Tornos' amongst others. The road descends steeply.

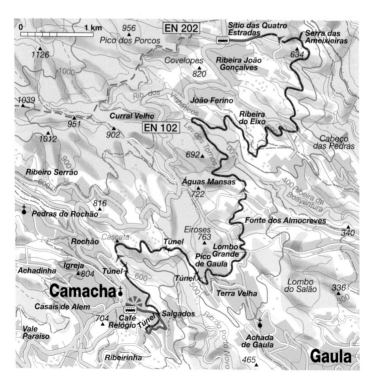

Hewn into the rock – the Levada dos Tornos below Camacha.

After 10 minutes you go right at the *Eira Salgada bar* down the cobbled road. 50m further on, just before the cobbled road goes between two houses look out for some steps on the right which take you to the *Levada dos Tornos*.

You will need your torch straight away for the 150m long tunnel downstream. A thick water pipe goes along the levada for a section.

Cross over a streambed and come to a second tunnel of just under 100m. Now the levada goes steeply across a rock face where the rock falls 50m vertically down right. Cross over a streambed at a waterfall on a boarded bridge.

There now follows a third tunnel of about 40m and 10m after that you come to another very murky looking tunnel. This time, however, you don't go through, but walk past it instead on the right with wonderful views of Camacha clinging to the upper edge of the Porto Novo valley. Some steps bring you up to the levada again.

As you walk on you cross two small roads and then in **Lombo Grande** you cross the EN 206 after a water tank. Continue along the levada and you now have a beautiful view of the Ponta de São Lourenço.

Cross over another road and you come to a short, low tunnel which requires you to stoop down as you walk through. The levada now runs into the valley of the **Ribeira dos Vinháticos** where there are some vertiginous sections to overcome. Go past a market garden and a water house and across two small roads going to João Ferino.

A new valley spreads out in front of you, but you cross over a road again and 2 minutes later you meet a cobbled path marked with a red dot. This path soon takes you uphill. But before that walk 4 minutes to the end of the *Levada dos Tornos* where it thunders down as a waterfall into a reservoir 200m below.

Turn round and go back to the cobbled path and climb up the rounded steps. At the electric cables follow the path to the left. You come to a cobbled road and you also go up left here. Pass the stone gateway of a Quinta on the right hand side.

10 minutes from the levada you cross over another cobbled road (if you follow it down to the right, it would bring you to Santo António da Serra). Straight on a bit further the path leads into an asphalt road which brings you to the crossroads **Sítio das Quatro Estradas**. The bus stop for Camacha is 40m on the right.

In the Ribeira dos Vinháticos valley.

16 Via Lamaceiros to Portela

Shady forest walk along the Levada da Serra

Sítio das Quatro Estradas – Lamaceiros forestry house – Portela

Starting point: from Funchal with No. 77 bus as far as the Sítio das Quatro Estradas bus stop, 750m.
Return: from Portela (670m) to Funchal with No. 53 bus.
Walking time: Sítio das Quatro Estradas – water house 1½ hrs, water house – Lamaceiros forestry house ½ hr, forestry house – Portela ¾ hr. Total time just under 2¾ hrs.
Ascent: 50 m, 140m in descent.
Grade: easy and shady levada walk on broad sign-posted forest path.
Refreshment: Miradouro da Portela restaurant and Portela à vista restaurant in Portela.
Linking tip: from Portela you can descend a cobbled path to Porto da Cruz (walk 17).

You can walk along the well-maintained and broad forest path to Portela all year round. Knotty oak trees line the path, the trunks are overgrown with moss and beard-moss hangs off the branches like lametta. A quiet, almost meditative stroll through the forest.

From the **Sítio das Quatro Estradas** bus stop follow the road from the crossroads to Poiso. Depending on the wind direction it can smell quite strange – behind the fence alongside the road there's a pig fattening farm. 10 minutes after the farm the *Levada da Serra*, situated at 800m, crosses the road. Follow this to the right. Straight away you will notice that the levada has no water left because it's no longer in use. However the broad path is still maintained.

At a **water house**, built in 1906, you come to a crossing of the paths (2km to the right takes you to Santo António da Serra). Continue straight on along the levada. Shortly afterwards the path gets narrower. You can get round this by going on the comfortable earth track which runs below the levada. After just under a quarter of an hour go straight over the crossroads where the levada flows through a small tunnel. 2 minutes afterwards you come to a forest road. Straight ahead goes to Ribeiro Frio, but you leave the levada here and take the forest road down to the right. You then reach the **Lamaceiros forestry house** in 10 minutes. There's a lovely picnic spot here under some tree ferns with tables and benches.

The rest of the walk will be familiar to walkers who have done the trout path (walk 19). Leave the forestry house on the left and follow the sign-posted forest road in the direction of Portela. After 200m the road forks at a view-point with tree ferns. Descend here to the left.

You now have your first glorious view of the north coast and Eagle Rock. After a sign-posted turn-off to the left you come past the farm of *Herdada Lombo das Faias* with a fence round it and the narrow *Levada da Portela* is now flowing close by.

Soon you can see the crossroads of Portela below. At the ruins of a house keep left down some steps and eventually you come to the EN 101. Follow this left for 200m to **Portela**. The bus stop is opposite the *Restaurant Portela à vista*.

Charred eucalyptus trees on the Levada da Serra after a forest fire.

17 Along the old cobbled path to Porto da Cruz

Descent to the north coast with wonderful views

Portela – Cruz da Guarda – Porto da Cruz

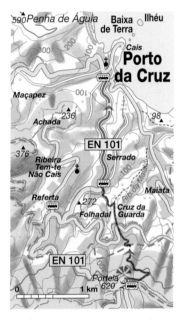

Starting point: from Funchal by car or with the No. 53 bus to Portela, 670m.

Return: from Porto da Cruz to Portela or Funchal also with the No. 53 bus.

Walking time: Portela – Cruz da Guarda ½ hr, Cruz da Guarda – Porto da Cruz 1 hr. Total time 1½ hrs.

Descent: 650m.

Grade: very steep descent on a cobbled path. Very slippery when wet.

Refreshment: restaurants in Porto da Cruz.

From the starting point in Portela you can see your destination quite clearly lying at your feet. The small port of Porto da Cruz is tucked into the eastern flank of Eagle Rock which dominates the coastal landscape. A well-maintained cobbled path with typically rounded steps brings you via the delightfully situated hamlet of Cruz da Guarda along a mountain ridge down to the sea.

From in front of the Miradouro da Portela restaurant in **Portela** take the tarmac path left of the entrance. At the following fork a broad path leads right through a break in the slope. However, keep to the left and turn onto the steeply descending old cobbled path about 150m from the restaurant. You quickly lose height and soon reach the hamlet of **Cruz da Guarda**.

The path meets the village road which you follow for 3 minutes and then turn left onto an asphalt road at the crossroads. The road curves round to the right and you go past a transformer station and after a bridge down some steps to a levada. A path by the channel runs below the road round a picturesque valley with long narrow terraces, acacias and a streambed overgrown with reeds.

Descent to Cruz da Guarda with a fantastic view of Eagle Rock.

The estate of Solar da Capela with its own chapel is above. 10 minutes from the road you meet the cobbled path again. Leave the levada and descend the cobbles to the right into another beautiful valley. The path loses its cobbles and you reach the EN 101 from where it's just under half an hour down to **Porto da Cruz**.

18 The 'belvedere' of Ribeiro Frio

To the spectacular vantage point in the misty wood

Ribeiro Frio – Balcões and back

Starting point: from Funchal by car or
No. 103 bus to Ribeiro Frio, 860m.
Walking time: Ribeiro Frio – Balcões
20 min, return 20 min. Total time 40 min.
Ascent: negligible.
Grade: easy stroll on a broad forest path,
slippery when wet.
Refreshment: two small bars on the way.
Linking tip: you can combine this short
walk with walks 19 and 20.

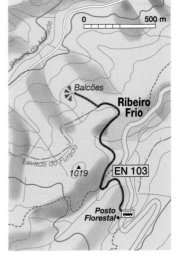

The shortest, but none-the-less rewarding walk on Madeira which
brings you to one of the most famous viewpoints of the island. The
path is therefore very busy. The qui-
etest time it is a weekday, before 11
o'clock in the morning if possible,
before the hoards of day trippers
completely take it over.

From the bus stop below the trout
farm in **Ribeiro Frio**, 20m after *Vic-
tor's Bar*, a broad path, sign-posted 'Balcões', branches off left from the
road. Straight away you are immersed in an enchanting fairy tale forest, with
tree trunks and rocks covered in moss and long beardmoss tumbling down
from the branches.

The channel leads through a small gorge. Go past two snack-bars, both
with wonderful views of the valley, and you come to a fork. The levada continues left (the path is closed to walkers). Follow the sign 'Balcões' to the
right and along a beautifully cobbled path you soon come to the **Balcões**
vantage point.

From here, in good weather, you can enjoy one of the most beautiful views
of the three highest peaks of the central massif. Pico do Gato (Cat Mountain) looks out from between Arieiro (left) and the jagged peaks of Pico das
Torres – Pico Ruivo is over to the right.

*From Balcões:
Pico do Gato (Cat Mountain) above the Fajã de Nogueira valley.*

19 Ribeiro Frio to Portela

Famous wet walk along the trout levada

Ribeiro Frio – Lamaceiros forestry house – Portela

Starting point: from Funchal by car or the No. 103 bus to Ribeiro Frio, 860m.
Return: from Portela (670m) to Funchal with No. 53 bus. If you have to return to your car, order a taxi in one of the restaurants in Portela.
Walking time: Ribeiro Frio – Lamaceiros water house 2½ hrs, water house – Lamaceiros forestry house 10 min, for-

estry house – Portela ¾ hr. Total time just under 3½ hrs.
Descent: just under 200m.
Grade: demanding levada walk on a broad path to start with, but then at times narrow and stony. Precipitous sections are protected with fences. In winter rainy and wet, in summer shady and cool.
Refreshment: two restaurants in Portela.

This classic levada walk is on almost every walking group's itinerary. The walk has everything which makes a levada walk interesting: clefts in the rocks, tunnels and in particular the luxuriant vegetation of a sub-tropical mountain forest. The almost all-year-round damp environment adds to the fascination. Rainbow trout dart through the levada, wagtails bob up and down in the 'cold river' and chaffinches peck at the crumbs left at picnic spots.

At *Victor's Bar* in **Ribeiro Frio** go a few steps down the road and at the yellow signpost »Portela 8km« (it is in fact a good 10km) turn off right and cross the bridge over the 'cold river'. Follow the broad path on the right hand bank and the *Levada do Furado* soon emerges next to you. Laurel and tree heathers form a dense roof-top, everywhere there's water dripping and gur-

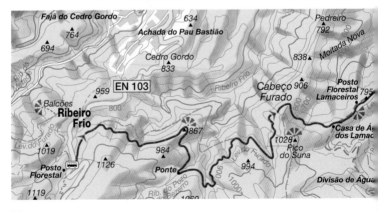

The state-run trout farm in Ribeiro Frio.

gling, rivulets and small waterfalls pour off the slopes. You can get round one particularly precipitous place protected with a wire fence without any

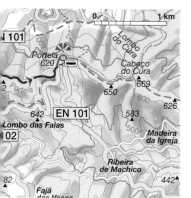

problems. Every now and then the laurel wood opens out to give views of the mountains. At times the path becomes so narrow that you have to balance along on the levada wall which is only 30cm wide.

After just under an hour you cross a concrete bridge over a stream. You have to circumnavigate two waterfalls by descending into the stony streambed.

Half an hour later the levada flows through an arch in the rock and another waterfall, 25m high, plunges down into the valley causing another slight detour.

The path forces its way in spectacular fashion through a rocky gorge and just under 10 minutes later you reach the first tunnel at the Cabeço Furado. Several tunnels, hewn into the rock and 3 to 6m long, follow one after the other and the rock face drops 100m steeply downwards.

20m after the **Lamaceiros water house** you come to a sign-posted path crossing. Leave the levada here and follow the broad path downhill in the direction of Portela. You soon meet a narrow channel again. At the **Lamaceiros forestry house** a picnic area under splendid fir trees and tree ferns is an inviting spot for a picnic.

Above: Rustic picnic spot at the Lamaceiros forestry house.
Left: The start of the path to the trout levada at Victor's Bar.

From the forestry house take the sign-posted forest road in the direction of Portela. At the fork after 200m descend left and look down onto the towering Eagle Rock by the coast.

After a sign-posted turn-off left you walk beside the narrow *Levada da Portela* past an estate with a fence round it. At the ruins of a house above Portela crossroads keep left down the steps to reach the EN 101.

Follow this left and after 200m you arrive at the **Portela** taxi rank and bus stop.

20 From Ribeiro Frio over the Feiteiras de Baixo plateau

Steep round walk in the laurel wood

Ribeiro Frio – Feiteiras de Baixo – Ribeiro Frio

Starting point: from Funchal by car or No. 103 bus to Ribeiro Frio, 860m.
Walking time: Ribeiro Frio – levada bridge 50 min, levada bridge – source of the levada 50 min, source of the levada – Chão das Feiteiras 25 min, Chão das Feiteiras – Ribeiro Frio 40 min. Total time 2¾ hrs.
Ascent: 300m, the same in descent.
Grade: ascent on steep paths, usually very wet all year round and slippery in places.
Difficult route finding in fog.
Refreshment: Victor's Bar in Ribeiro Frio is the specialist restaurant for fresh trout – fried, grilled or smoked.

Linking tip: you can combine this walk with walk 18.

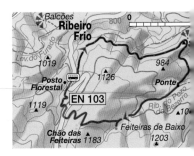

The walk round Ribeiro Frio can degenerate into a really damp experience as the route goes through one of the regions with the highest rainfall on Madeira. At first it follows a section of the *Levada do Furado* in the direction of Portela and then on a narrow path it climbs up to the plateau at almost 1200m. A walk not often done, but one where it's worth getting wet.

In **Ribeiro Frio** at *Victor's Bar* go a few paces down the street and turn onto the cobbled path with the yellow signpost 'Portela 8km'. Below the restaurant cross the Ribeiro Frio on a bridge and soon the *Levada do Furado* emerges next to you. As in walk 19 follow the pretty channel at first for a good 50 minutes as far as the concrete **levada bridge**. Narrow side channels pour into the levada to the right of the bridge. Leave the Portela path here and climb 2m up to the side levada which comes from above.

Climb up very steeply beside the narrow channel on steps which are usually slippery even in summer. After a quarter of an hour the steepest section is over and another 15 minutes after that the levada narrows for a few metres to a gutter only 6 inches wide.

Here a path turns off right up some steps at the point where the levada is usually covered in branches. But first of all go another 25m straight ahead to the **source of the levada**. In dry weather the pools in front of cascading waterfalls make an idyllic place to stop.

Crystal clear pools at the source of the levada.

Go back the 25m from the source of the levada and then turn up left onto the path, overgrown in places with ferns and scrub. In the middle of this green jungle you come to a circular clearing full of ferns. Go straight through the ferns, crossing over several goat paths on the way. Route finding is especially difficult here when it's foggy and it's best then to turn round and go back.

The path leads up to a rounded hilltop covered in heather and bilberry bushes. The buildings of **Chão das Feiteiras** (1170m) lie ahead. There are hardly any paths through the sheep pasture towards the houses. In front of the houses you meet a broad grassy path which you follow to the right. After a good 200m turn left down onto the old Madeira path. The rounded cobble stones shine through from below the ferns, grass and moss.

You eventually reach the EN 103 where the cobbled path was interrupted for a section. Following the road down right you come to the cobbled path again after a bend. The water supply for the trout farm cascades downwards beside you. At the picnic area around the fish pools and the **Ribeiro Frio** forestry house you meet the EN 103 again which brings you back to *Victor's Bar* in 200m.

21 Fajã da Nogueira

The tunnel path from the hydroelectric power plant to the Levada do Pico Ruivo

Fajã da Nogueira – Levada do Pico Ruivo – Pico Ruivo tunnel and back

Starting point: by car from Funchal via Poiso into the Ribeira da Fajã da Nogueira valley. Shortly before Cruzinhas a 4km long unsurfaced roadway branches off to the Fajã da Nogueira hydroelectric power plant (620m).

Walking time: Fajã da Nogueira hydroelectric power plant – Montado do Sabugal ¾ hr, Montado do Sabugal – Levada do Pico Ruivo ¼ hr, levada – Pico Ruivo tunnel ¾ hr, return 1¾ hrs. Total time 3½ hrs.

Ascent: 400m, the same in descent.

Grade: easy walk on roadways and levada paths with a slight ascent. A torch is necessary for the tunnel.

Refreshment: no facilities on the way.

Alternative route: intrepid tunnel and long distance walkers can go through the 2.4km Pico Ruivo tunnel to Cadeirão do Inferno and Caldeirão Verde (walks 25 and 26) and if need be descend via Queimadas/Pico das Pedras to Santana. You should allow 40 minutes for the tunnel

– don't forget to put in some spare batteries!

The hydroelectric power plant in the Ribeira da Fajã da Nogueira valley makes a significant contribution to the Madeira's energy supply. On the *Levada do Pico Ruivo*, peppered with tunnels, you can get a sense of the magnificent mountains of the region. The channel takes the water from Caldeirão do Inferno (Hell's Cauldron) through the numerous tunnels to the hydroelectric power plant.

The walk begins 80m in front of the **Fajã hydroelectric power plant**. At the same height as some steps going up to a group of houses turn off right from the approach road to the hydroelectric power plant onto a roadway. A sign 'Parque Natural da Madeira' gives you advance notice of the Ribeira da Fajã da Nogueira valley which belongs to the nature reserve. The track leads a long way into the valley and on the left you see a thick pipe coming down from Pico da Nogueira. At a clearing (sign '**Montado do Sabugal**') you come past two huge laurel trees, the roots of which go back to the time when Madeira was discovered. 2 minutes later the path divides and you take the right fork and continue ascending past magnificent laurel trees up to the **Levada do Pico Ruivo** on 1000m. The channel is at first covered over with slabs and you follow it to the right.

After eight smaller tunnels of no more than 20m in length you need a torch to help you through the ninth and tenth tunnel. Rusty rails from a disused tipper lorry railway run into the eleventh tunnel. The darkness is punctuated at the end of this tunnel by 5 series of windows. After the first window a secondary levada flows in from the right. At the end of the tunnel you come to the Ribeira Seco riverbed where it has carved out a ravine of just a few metres and is almost totally filled in with scree. Two waterfalls roar down into the valley. The rails go on pipes laid across the streambed into the 2.4km long **Pico Ruivo tunnel**. An enchanted spot – turn round in front of the entrance to the tunnel.

The tunnel path along the Levada Pico Ruivo.

The north coast

The climate of Madeira's wildly romantic north side is characterised by a lot of rain and clouds and little sun. When the sun does get through the natural landscape appears even more delightful. The coastal mountains drop away steeply and rivers crash into the sea in the form of waterfalls.

Porto da Cruz is tucked away at the foot of the massive Eagle Rock. In former times sugar cane was shipped from the tiny harbour and the chimney of a sugar factory brings back memories of Madeira's age of 'white gold'. A sea-water pool, rescued from the stormy Atlantic waves, provides the opportunity for a swim.

Faial lies on the west side of Eagle Rock in the middle of a sprawling, in Madeiran terms at least, valley plain. Its pilgrims' church is the focal point for a large annual pilgrimage. Wine, fruit and vegetables are cultivated all round the village and many smallholders sell their produce at the roadside. From a vantage point on the road up to Santana you can enjoy marvellous views of the north coast as far as the São Lourenço peninsula in the furthest northeast.

Santana is famous for its traditional pointed gable houses. The reed-thatched roofs reach right down to the ground and painted doors and windows radiate colour from the triangular façades. The confined living space of the Santana cottages has caused most inhabitants to move into new accommodation. Thus many cottages are threatened with collapse. In order to protect this traditional country architecture quite a lot of the archetypal houses have been cleaned out to provide an open-air museum. This central village on the north coast is the starting point for walks into the huge rock basins of Caldeirão Verde and Caldeirão do Inferno and it's only a stone's throw via Achada do Teixeira to Pico Ruivo, the roof of Madeira.

Behind Santana an exposed road links together the few villages in the north. An original eye-catcher is the **São Vicente** chapel nestling into the rocks in an estuary. Other sights here are the lava caves. You can explore 700m of the extensive volcanic cavities which were formed 400.000 years ago on a guided tour.

Experienced drivers should not miss out on the spectacular section of road between São Vicente and Porto Moniz. The road narrows to a single lane in places and winds in between steep rock faces and cliff edges and waterfalls splash onto the roof of your car to provide a free car wash.

The 'waterfall shower' along the path to Caldeirão do Inferno.

22 To the source of the Levada do Castelejo

Opposite Eagle Rock into the Ribeira de São Roque valley

Cruz – source of the Levada do Castelejo and back

Starting point: from Funchal with No. 53 bus to Cruz, 240m, or by car from Porto da Cruz in the direction of Faial as far as Cruz. At the sign for the village at the highest point of the ridge a little road branches off to the left (difficult to park, better to follow the road uphill for a little way and then stop on the right).

Walking time: Cruz – source of the Levada do Castelejo 1½ hrs, return 1½ hrs. Total time 3 hrs.

Ascent: Just under 100m.

Grade: easy levada walk, but you need a good head for heights – some sections are unprotected.

Refreshment: no facilities on the way.

Alternative route: you can also begin the walk in Referta. From the bus stop on the EN 101 go 20m along the road to Achada and go down to the levada at the steps.

The walking time is about 2½ hrs longer.

The picturesque hamlet of Cruz lies on a mountain ridge between Porto da Cruz and Faial. This very beautiful route goes through a green valley along the *Levada do Castelejo* at the upper edge of the settlement boundary. After views of Eagle Rock it brings you into the unspoiled Ribeira de São Roque valley. This walk is in the shade for long stretches at a time and even in summer the sun does not reach the deeply-cut valley bottom at the source until about midday.

At the village sign in **Cruz** turn off from the EN 101 onto a small road and follow it through the village over the mountain ridge. At a small chest-high water house after a good 10 minutes you meet the *Levada do Castelejo* which flows underneath the little road. Follow the levada upstream to the right. With a view of Eagle Rock it now goes through traditional farmland and corncobs lie out on the roofs to dry after the harvest.

After about 30 minutes the levada forks off left into the Ribeira de São Roque valley. You can see the picturesque village of São Roque on a rocky mountain ridge opposite. The further you go into the valley, the more unspoiled the vegetation becomes. Magnificent lilac Morning Glory entwine themselves high around the trunks of pine and acacia trees. The valley gets narrower and you make your way slowly down to the riverbed and reach a point where the levada comes out from under an enormous boulder. From here you hop the last few metres to the **source of the levada** (330m) through the stony streambed. On the left hand side of the pools you can walk a little further up the river on a rocky mountain path and enjoy a pleasant rest on one of the boulders amidst rushing waterfalls.

In the source area of the Levada do Castelejo.

23 Up onto Eagle Rock, 590m

Demanding path onto the symbol of Madeira's north coast

Penha de Águia de Baixo – Penha de Águia and back

Starting point: go by car from Faial towards Porto da Cruz. In the valley after the bridge turn off left to the hamlet of Penha de Águia de Baixo (150m). You can park at the Galé restaurant. If you are travelling by bus go as far as Faial and then walk from there for just under 3km to the starting point.

Walking time: Penha de Águia de Baixo – western summit ¾ hr, western summit – Penha de Águia ½ hr, return 1 hr. Total time 2¼ hrs.

Ascent: 440m, the same in descent.

Grade: strenuous steep ascent on stony mule tracks. The path is at times difficult to find and demands a certain measure of route finding.

Refreshment: Galé restaurant at the start of the path.

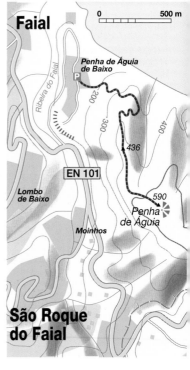

The massive form of Eagle Rock makes it a landmark which can be seen on the north coast from a long way off. The rock gets its name from the many ospreys which used to nest here. This huge mass of rock falls away precipitously on all sides and you would hardly expect a path to go up across the rock face onto the flat summit plateau. And even though the walk is very strenuous it is extremely rewarding.

In **Penha de Águia de Baixo** right next to the *Galé restaurant* go right, up the five steps of a house entrance which has a small knee-high wall round it. The path behind the house goes through vineyards and is fairly overgrown. Make straight for a white-washed *barn* above with a rusty red roof. Continue to ascend up diagonally to the left and a minute later keep straight ahead up some steep steps.

The path is very exposed here in places. After a short flat section where you can regain your breath you reach the north flank. Through at first dense

The massive Eagle Rock is the symbol of the north coast.
In the foreground is the village of Faial; on the left behind the rock the peninsula of
São Lourenço pushes far out to the east.

bushes of heather the now distinct path enters a splendid pine forest with six feet high ferns.

Once you've arrived at the south ridge the path forks. You can see the Faial valley through the tops of the pine trees. Along the path on the right you come in one minute onto the **western summit** where there's only a limited view because of the trees.

Back at the fork a marvellous ridge path heads eastwards with views over the valley and the central massif. At times rather overgrown and extremely steep it is sometimes necessary to scramble over fallen tree trunks. Then quite suddenly you find yourself at the trig point of the **Penha de Águia** – but be careful here because the rock really does fall away as steeply as it looks from below. To the south over the terraced valley there's an impressive view of the chain of mountains of the central massif.

As soon as you have regained your breath continue following the path for another 100m further east to a rewarding vantage point of the north coast as far as Ponta de São Lourenço.

24 The coastal path from Santana to São Jorge

Coastal walk on old cobbled paths with beautiful views

Santana – Quinta do Furão – Calhau – Caes – São Jorge

Starting point: by car or bus to Santana, 330m. Coming from Funchal don't get off at the town hall, go another 1.7km in the direction of São Jorge as far as the Bragado's Pub bus stop.
Return: No. 103 bus from São Jorge back to the starting point or to Funchal.
Walking time: Santana – Quinta do Furão ¼ hr, Quinta do Furão – Calhau ¾ hr, Calhau – Caes ¼ hr, Caes – São Jorge 50 min. Total time a good 2 hrs.
Descent: 350m, 300m in ascent.
Grade: steep descent and ascent on cobbled paths.
For the detour to the old harbour you need to be sure-footed and have a head for heights.
In Calhau there are opportunities for swimming.

Refreshment: Neptunos Bar in Calhau.

The cobbled path between Santana and São Jorge is threatened with collapse since the new road has been built. But although it has broken away in many places it's still quite possible to walk along this old link path. The section of path to the boat mooring is spectacular where it is hewn into the rocks right above the rolling waves.

From the bus stop at *Bragado's Pub* in **Santana** go 100m along the EN 101 towards São Jorge and then turn right onto a small road going uphill. The cobbled path goes round a ruined estate on a right hand bend. Past a water tank it joins the approach road of the **Quinta do Furão** hotel which stands like a grand castle in the middle of vineyards.

Follow the approach road to the left and after 15m turn into the road coming from Santana. This brings you up a gentle incline through vineyards to a hill with a stand of pine trees. Turn left there onto a path leading to a house. Past the house it becomes recognisable as the old cobbled path and zigzags towards the sea, in places overgrown with grass. You soon have a beautiful view of Calhau beach and the zigzag path going up from there to São Jorge.

When you arrive in the valley bottom cross the riverbed of the Ribeira de São Jorge over an old arched bridge. At **Calhau** shingle beach you can go for an invigorating swim either in the open sea or in the protected small lagoon. Past *Neptunos Bar* you come to a well at which point you go uphill to São Jorge. But first follow the coastal path straight ahead and go past the delapidated ruins of Calhau. It's hard to believe that the village was for several years one of the most important harbours on the north coast.

The path, hewn into the rock, now runs for 10 to 15 minutes above the sea. Parts of the path have broken away and sometimes it narrows to only a metre wide. After a waterfall made green with Taro leaves there's a section where you need to have a head for heights.

You can now see the old ships' mooring (**Caes**) at the basalt promontory sticking out into the sea like a bridge. Unfortunately the last part of the path is totally broken away and only with a bit of climbing can you manage to reach the makeshift wooden bridge to the mole which the local fishermen use, but which is rather dangerous for those not used to it.

So return to the well and go up the cobbled path to São Jorge. After a 40 minute steep ascent you come to a road. The cobbled path continues diagonally opposite and brings you to the cemetery in 4 minutes. A road leads from there up to **São Jorge**.

At a chapel surrounded by three palm trees you meet the village road where you continue straight on uphill to the *Igreja São Jorge*, one of the most beautiful baroque churches on Madeira. The bus stop is 30m before the church.

The wooden footbridge to Calhau quay is only recommended to adventurous walkers.

25 Caldeirão Verde

From the ranch into the green basin

Rancho Madeirense – Queimadas – Caldeirão Verde and back

Starting point: coming from Faial turn left after the Shell petrol station in Santana towards Pico Ruivo and follow the little road 6km as far as the car park of the Rancho Madeirense, 880m.

If you are travelling by bus take a taxi from Santana to the Rancho Madeirense and order it for the return from there.

Walking time: Rancho Madeirense – Parque Queimadas ½ hr, Parque Queimadas – Vale da Lapa turn-off 1¼ hrs, Vale da Lapa turn-off – Caldeirão Verde ½ hr, return 2½ hrs. Total time just under 4½ hrs.

Ascent: negligible.

Grade: the comfortable levada path, broad at first, gets narrower during the course of the walk and sometimes you have to balance along small and narrow walls of 30cm.

Precipitous sections are protected with wire fences, but you still need a good head for heights.

In winter the loamy path can be wet and slippery with draining rivulets. A torch is necessary for the tunnels.

Refreshment: Snack-bar at the Rancho Madeirense.

Alternative route: from Queimadas you can descend a small road in 1½ hrs to Santana.

Linking tip: you can walk from Caldeirão Verde to Caldeirão do Inferno (see walk 26).

The walk into the green basin is one of the most spectacular levada walks on the island. During the course of evolution the water created not only impressive gorges, but was also responsible for the jungle-like evergreen vegetation. The levada has for the most part been cut into a rock face and it seems incredible that trees and bushes manage to cling to the vertical slopes. At the end of the walk an imposing waterfall plunges into a small lake where hardy types can go for an invigorating swim.

From the car park at **Rancho Madeirense** leave the small reed-thatched Santana house on your left hand side and at the reception for the ranch go straight ahead along the broad earth track. The *Levada do Caldeirão* is at first hidden under slabs, but through the gaps you can see that you are

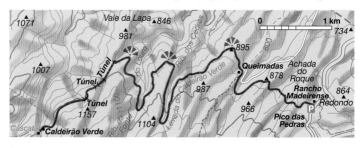

walking upstream. Splendid Hydrangeas line both sides of the levada.

Keeping on the main path, at a picnic spot you cross a babbling stream over a bridge and soon afterwards the cobbled road at the **Parque das Queimadas**. Past two straw-thatched houses you come to a duck pond and a wooden bridge. Beyond there's a sign which says 'Caldeirão Verde 6.5km'. The path becomes narrow. Due to the dense undergrowth at the side of the path which lessens the effect, some precipitous places of up to 100m do not appear too vertiginous. Soon you catch a glimpse of the north coast and deep below in the valley on a plateau lies the idyllic hamlet of Ilha.

Santana cottage at the start of the walk to Caldeirão Verde in Pico das Pedras.

At an impassable narrow point you go round the levada along a path to the right. The levada then runs into a side valley and is channeled over a small gorge on an elegant bridge. You come across a waterfall pouring down into the levada from a height of 50m. You can easily cross the streambed in front of the waterfall. There are now some vertiginous sections well-protected with wire cables. Go through a tunnel which, although only 20m long, is pitch-black with a bend in the middle.

10 minutes later you reach the turn-off to **Vale da Lapa** in front of the second tunnel. Go straight on through the tunnel, about 200m long, which may sometimes be wet under foot. You have hardly had time to get accustomed to the daylight before you arrive at the third tunnel. It has an invitingly large entrance, but soon turns out to be narrow and low. However in the middle there's a beautiful series of windows.

After the fourth short tunnel the levada flows into the magnificent gorge of the Ribeira Grande. In front of an overflow leave the levada on a rocky path up to the left and you soon find yourself in the **Caldeirão Verde**, an impressive basin of vertical walls with a waterfall cascading down from a height of a good 100m.

26 Into the Devil's Cauldron Caldeirão do Inferno

A superlative trip full of adventure

Caldeirão Verde – Caldeirão do Inferno and back

Starting point: the walk is only possible in conjunction with walk 25. Start in Caldeirão Verde.

Walking time: Caldeirão Verde – source of the Levada do Caldeirão ½ hr, source – Pico Ruivo tunnel 10 min, Pico Ruivo tunnel – Caldeirão do Inferno 25 min, return to the Caldeirão Verde ¾ hr. Total time 1 hr 50 min plus 4½ hrs for the walk to and from the Caldeirão Verde.

Ascent: 80m.

Grade: the walk on from Caldeirão Verde is only for experienced levada walkers and recommended for the summer months. The vertiginous levada path is not protected and the steps up to Pico Ruivo tunnel can often be extremely slippery. A torch is necessary for the numerous tunnels.

Refreshment: no facilities on the way.

Linking tip: you can descend through the 2.4km long Pico Ruivo tunnel to the Fajã da Nogueira hydroelectric power plant (walk 21 in reverse). Don't forget spare batteries for your torch!

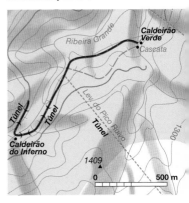

The path from the 'Green Cauldron' into the 'Devil's Cauldron' is one of the most fascinating levada walks on Madeira. It is difficult to understand to what purpose this ingenious system of channels has been laid into an almost impenetrable mountain region. Waterfalls, tunnels, canyons and a huge basin-shaped valley are the highlights of this vertiginous walk.

From **Caldeirão Verde** continue following the *Levada do Caldeirão*. After 4 minutes you come to a break in the walk where there's a wonderful view into the Ribeira Grande gorge and its stony streambed.

For a good quarter of an hour you continue along the extremely precipitous levada to an impassable section which you can get round by descending and then ascending some steps. 4 minutes later on the left you pass some steps that have been cut into the rock. Climb up here to the *Levada do Pico Ruivo* on the next level. Before that you can continue straight ahead to the **source of the Levada do Caldeirão** and admire the marvellous waterfall that feeds it.

Back at the steps, which are almost always wet, climb for 7 minutes up to **Pico Ruivo tunnel**, 80m higher, and see the waterfall in its fullness again.

Take the right hand tunnel entrance and go immediately right through a 5m long side tunnel beside a pool protected with a wire fence. 50m after the pool you are standing in front of a tunnel where a waterfall splashes down onto the levada path. Depending on the weather you will be subjected to either a heavy or a light shower, but in summer it's not a problem in getting through (see photo p. 85).

Following this relatively short tunnel there's one of about 150m. After that you should keep an eye on the precipice next to the levada. Another tunnel is low at first (watch your head) and has four windows. There's a gentle incline at the end of the tunnel, the levada flowing with a deafening roar beside you, and the drone of waterfalls can be heard ahead.

Leave the tunnel up a few steps and you find yourself standing at one of the most spectacular spots on Madeira. The Ribeira Grande has created a narrow ravine here. Two wooden bridges covered with branches lead across and two waterfalls plunge down into the levada. After the second bridge you need to go through a narrow entrance (not for large people or big rucksacks) into a tunnel of about 80m in length. After three more tunnels you eventually reach the awesome **Caldeirão do Inferno**. The vertically high walls are in fact not as narrow as the Caldeirão Verde, but are twice as high.

Go back the same way to the **Caldeirão Verde**.

Lime green pools in front of the steep wall of Caldeirão do Inferno.

Central Madeira and Curral das Freiras

Madeira's reputation as a walkers' paradise is founded not only on its marvellous levada paths. The centre of the island is dominated by an alpine-like massif, the highest summits of which reach almost 1900m. The backbone of the island is of volcanic origin and rose up out of the sea 20 million years ago. The erosive power of wind and rain has formed bizarre jagged rocks and torrents of water have created deep gorges. The soft layers of tufa were washed away and left behind exposed rock tunnels of hard basalt through weathering.

A panoramic road runs right into the heart of the mountain area up to **Pico do Arieiro**, at 1818m the third highest peak on the island. It's only a few steps from the panoramic restaurant up to the summit column where you can enjoy a magnificent view of the primeval scenery divided by rock towers, ridges and valleys. A well-constructed high mountain path (walk 28) links the three highest peaks with one another in most spectacular fashion – the walk is a must for every hiker.

From Pico do Arieiro you can also cast your gaze down to **Curral das Freiras**. The 'corral of the nuns' got its name from an order of sisters from the Santa Clara monastery who fled into the isolated valley over winding mountain paths in 1566 to escape Funchal pirates.

Romantic dawn: sunrise at Miradouro Ninho da Manta, on the right the Pico do Arieiro.

Spectacular section on Pico das Torres.

Originally it was thought that the valley in the shape of a basin was a volcanic crater, but geologists have proved that this basin, surrounded by Madeira's highest peaks, has been formed by the erosive force of the Curral river over a period of millions of years.

Only since 1959 has Curral das Freiras been linked to the island's road network and its electricity supply started in 1962. The old, partly paved descent paths into the basin are all still well-preserved and make the Nuns' Valley an interesting destination for a walk.

27 **Via Achada do Teixeira onto Pico Ruivo, 1862m**

Airy ascent onto the highest peak on the island

Achada do Teixeira – Pico Ruivo and back

Starting point: in Santana at the Shell petrol station follow the signs for 'Pico Ruivo' and after 14km via Pico das Pedras you come to the car park at the Archada do Teixeira, 1592m. The road is open daily from 7.00 until 21.00 – there's a barrier across the road at night at Pico das Pedras.
Go by bus as far as Santana and take a taxi from there to the Achada.
Walking time: Achada do Teixeira – Pico Ruivo 1 hr, return ¾ hr. Total time 1¾ hrs.
Ascent: 270m, the same in descent.
Grade: in fine weather this is an easy high mountain walk. The path is cobbled almost throughout, except for the 10 minute stony summit path.
The region is often cloudy and strong winds can often get up quickly as well.
Refreshment: drinks are on sale in the Pico Ruivo mountain hut.
Linking tips: you can combine a walk from Pico Ruivo to Pico do Arieiro (walk 28) and to Encumeada pass (walk 30). You can also descend into the Nuns' Valley (walk 37).
Alternative route: back at the Achada you can descend via Queimadas to Santana. There's a path down past the Homem em Pé which meets the approach

road to the Achada and 2 minutes later the viewpoint. Follows this downhill as far as Queimadas. In Queimadas continue down a narrow cobbled road to Santana. You need to allow 3 hours for the 1200m descent.

Madeira's highest mountain is open to everyone – a comfortable cobbled path makes the ascent almost into a stroll of under an hour. Of course you can't expect to stand all by yourself at the summit cross. Even the grazing sheep have be-

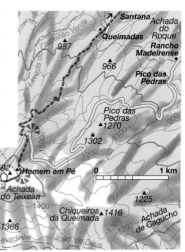

The 'stone man' Homem em Pé on the Achada doTeixeira.

come accustomed to the numerous summiteers and are more confident here than anywhere else.

Begin the walk by taking a short detour to the *Homem em Pé*. From the car park at the **Achada do Teixeira** head towards the hut. A path fenced-off on both sides leads to the right past the hut. After 1 or 2 minutes turn left and already you will see the striking rock formation ahead (10 minutes there and back).

Back at the car park the signpost 'Pico Ruivo' points the way to the summit ascent. 30m after the sign the unmistakable cobbled path starts over the sustained mountain ridge. From the first hut at the latest you can enjoy fabulous views of Pico do Arieiro and back to the north coast as far as the Ponta de São Lourenço in the east.

From the second hut you can now see Pico Ruivo as well and the hut below it. You come past a third hut and just below the Pico Ruivo mountain hut you meet the path which comes over from Pico do Arieiro (walk 28).

Go up right for 2 minutes to reach the *Pico Ruivo mountain hut*, built in 1939. Go past the well and the little WC shed and continue climbing up the steps. At the turn-off 5 minutes later keep to the left and after a short stony ascent of 10 minutes you will reach the summit column of **Pico Ruivo**. An amazing 360-degree-panorama – the whole island lies at your feet.

28 From Pico do Arieiro onto Pico Ruivo, 1862m

An excellent walk onto the roof of Madeira

Pico do Arieiro – Pico Ruivo and back

Starting point: by car or taxi via Poiso to the car park at Pico do Arieiro, 1818m. No public transport.
Walking time: Pico do Arieiro – Pico do

Gato tunnel ¾ hr, Pico do Gato tunnel – Pico das Torres tunnel 1¼ hrs, Pico das Torres tunnel – Pico Ruivo mountain hut ½ hr, mountain hut – Pico Ruivo ¼ hr, Pico Ruivo – Pico das Torres tunnel ½ hr, Pico das Torres tunnel – Pico do Arieiro 1½ hrs. Total time 4¾ hrs.
Descent: about 600m, 800m in ascent.
Grade: very demanding high mountain walk on partly cobbled, partly stony mule tracks. Only makeshift protection on precipitous sections. Fitness is required for the steep ascents and a torch for the tunnels.
Tip: landslides sometimes make the path impassable, so find out beforehand if both paths are passable. The path is closed when there's snow and ice.
Refreshment: restaurant at Pico do Arieiro, drinks on sale in the Pico Ruivo mountain hut.
Alternative routes: if you don't need to return to your car descend via Achada do Teixeira and continue to Santana (see walk 27). Long distance walkers can stay overnight in the Pico Ruivo mountain hut (only by prior notification) and from there walk to the Encumeada pass (walk 30) or into the Nuns' Valley (walk 37).

There is not a more exciting high mountain walk on Madeira. The mountain path, constructed a good 30 years ago by the island administration, links the three highest mountains with each other in spectacular fashion. For this walk you should make an early start as gathering clouds shroud the summit around midday.

From the car park at **Pico do Arieiro** leave the restaurant on the right hand side and go up the steps past some souvenir shops to the summit column.

Descent from Arieiro to the 'buzzard's nest'.

After orientating yourself for a while on Pico do Arieiro follow the yellow signpost 'Pico Ruivo' 20m below the summit down the cobbled path. A quarter of an hour later you reach the *Miradouro Ninho da Manta* (the 'buzzard's nest') from where there's a magnificent view down into the Ribeira da Fajã da Nogueira valley below.

A short climb over a spectacular rock tower brings you to another viewing balcony. The rest of the walk around the east flank of Pico das Torres can be clearly seen ahead. Descend a section of path that is protected with wire cables to **Pico do Gato tunnel**. The path divides just after the 50m long, mostly wet tunnel. Choose the right hand fork through the gate (the 'tunnel path' from the left is where you'll return).

A level section follows and after the sign 'Fontes' you begin the 25 minute ascent over some eroded steps up the east flank of Pico das Torres. Go through a gate and at a notch you can catch a glimpse of the north coast and Eagle Rock. From the notch descend on a stony path from Pico das Torres in a good 10 minutes.

Keeping height you contour round several valley clefts until you meet the 'tunnel path' again at the exit from **Pico das Torres tunnel**. Do not go through the gate in front of the tunnel, instead keep to the right. After just under 10 minutes a well-trodden path leads onto a rock projection covered in

Above: The Pico Ruivo mountain hut sits in an exposed position on a rock projection.
Left: A walk to Pico Ruivo, an excellent walk, offering a bumper bundle of alpine climbs.

gnarled heather where you can take a pleasant rest with views down to Faial.

After another ascent and a goat gate you meet the cobbled path below the Ruivo hut which comes up from Achada do Teixeira (walk 27) and 2 minutes later, you reach the **Pico Ruivo mountain hut**.

Now begins the last stage up to the island's highest peak past the well and the little WC shed. At the turn-off 5 minutes later keep to the left and after a short steep ascent you are standing at the summit column of **Pico Ruivo** (1862m).

From the summit return on the now familiar path to **Pico das Torres tunnel**. Choose here the somewhat shorter and less exhausting 'tunnel path' to Arieiro through the gate and the 40m long tunnel. The mule track, daringly cut into the rock, runs through several small tunnels and one of about 200m in length. Keeping height the path runs across the steep rock face of Pico das Torres below partly overhanging rock. Precipitous places are poorly protected.

Before Pico do Gato tunnel you meet the path you came up on and you return along this through the tunnel and via both belvederes to **Pico do Arieiro**.

29 From the Poço da Neve to Funchal

Descent with wonderful views from the high mountains into the capital

Poço da Neve – Levada da Negra – Barreira

Starting point: by car or taxi follow the road via Poiso up to Pico do Arieiro. The start of the path is 1.8km before Arieiro on the left hand side of the road at the igloo-shaped Poço da Neve snow house, 1650m. If you stayed overnight in the Pousada walk the 1.8km to the snow house.

Walking time: Poço da Neve – Levada da Negra ½ hr, Levada da Negra – water house 1 hr 20 min, water house – Barreira 40 min. Total time 2½ hrs.

Descent: 900m.

Grade: long descent on partly stony paths, a head for heights would not go amiss.

Refreshment: no facilities on the way.

Alternative route: if you have to return to the car, turn round at the sheep pen.

Linking tip: for long distance walkers there's an opportunity to combine the descent into the capital with walks 28 and 30 (in reverse).

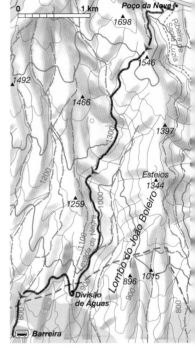

The Poço da Neve snow house is a relic from the time when there was no refrigeration. In winter the precious ice was carried in leather bags, packed in straw, down to Funchal. The short-lived cargo was coveted as much in hospitals as a cooling agent as in the kitchen of the Reid's luxury hotel where it was served up in the form of sorbets. The old path along the *Levada da Negra* is the shortest descent from the central massif into the capital and leads through the newest environmentally protected Parque Ecológico.

At the sign for the **Poço da Neve** go through the gate down to the snow house ('stone igloo'). Below it at the fork take the left hand path and first of all keep heading towards the transmitter masts. The path runs through meadows of ferns and tall-stemmed bilberry bushes and meets a broad stony path which you follow straight on downhill.

From the Poço da Neve 'stone igloo' you can see 1650m down to Funchal.

The path goes round a right hand bend into the Ribeira de Santa Luzia valley. After a gate you cross the streambed on stepping stones. On the other side, along an indistinct path at first, you head straight for a striking rock formation on the mountain ridge. There you meet the 6 inch wide channel of the **Levada da Negra** which you follow downstream. Soon you can see below on the right circular sheep pens on the plateau of *Terreiro Fecho*. At this point the levada begins to slope down steeply. Cross a path and after a few steps you see on the opposite river bank another levada which, a few minutes later, is channelled over a steel girder and joins your levada.

Cross the streambed and from above left another narrower channel joins the levada which, with its tributaries, is now almost double in size. The levada flows on the right hand bank into a v-shaped valley and the stony riverbed soon lies far below. A fire raged years ago in the valley below on the left and there still remain charred tree trunks strewn all over the slope like matches.

Through an eucalyptus wood you reach a **water house** at a levada crossing. Keep diagonally right (left goes to Trapiche). 20 minutes after the water house the levada meets a cobbled path. Continue to descend down this path and you are soon above the roofs of Funchal. São Martinho church is very striking and the tower appears to be standing above the sea. The cobbled path turns into a concrete path leading down steeply to meet the asphalt road in **Barreira** (750m) which ends in a turning circle . There's a bus stop here for the No. 10 local bus to bring you down into the centre of Funchal.

30 Over Pico Ruivo to the Encumeada pass

Superlative ridge walk over the meteorological divide of Madeira

Achada do Teixeira – Pico Ruivo – Boca das Torrinhas – Encumeada pass

Starting point: from Santana by taxi to the Achada do Teixeiro, 1592m.

Return: No. 6 bus bus from the Encumeada pass to Funchal.

Walking time: Achada do Teixeira – Pico Ruivo 1 hr, Pico Ruivo – Boca das Torrinhas 1¾ hrs, Boca das Torrinhas – Encumeada pass 2 hrs 20 min. Total time a good 5 hrs.

Ascent: 500m and a good 1000m in descent.

Grade: 18km long and a demanding high mountain walk with steep ascents and descents. The partly stony path is marked throughout with yellow and red diamond-shaped signs.

Refreshment: drinks on sale in the Pico Ruivo mountain hut. Snack-bar at the Encumeada pass.

Alternative route 1: fit walkers can drive to the Encumeada pass and do the walk from there as far as Pico Ruivo and return to the pass. In this way you avoid the tedious journey via Santana. See walk 37 for the start from Boca da Encumeada. You should allow at least 8 hrs for the walk to and from Pico Ruivo. It's a good 1000m in ascent and descent.

Alternative route 2: from Boca das Torrinhas you can descend into the Nuns' Valley (walk 37) and there's a good bus service to Funchal from there.

The ridge path to the Encumeada pass is one of the big alpine mountain walks on Madeira and you should not be put off by the tedious access. The delightful thing about this path is the way it changes over several times from one side of the ridge to the other and affords views first of the north coast and then the south coast to Curral and Ribeira Brava. Sections of the path in between are overgrown with dense heather and now and then the thick canopy of trees lets through a scattering of diffuse light.

Descent from Pico Ruivo to the east-west ridge of the central massif.

From the car park at the **Achada do Teixeira** it's an easy ascent up the steps over the sustained mountain ridge to Pico Ruivo. From the first refuge at the latest you can enjoy wonderful views of the Ariero and back to the

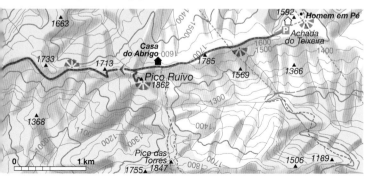

north coast as far as the São Lourenço peninsula in the east. After passing some more shelters you reach the *Pico Ruivo mountain hut*. Next to the hut you can refresh your drink bottles from a well. Continue climbing up the steps at the well and in 5 minutes reach the turn-off to the summit. If you don't want to go up to **Pico Ruivo** (20 minutes there and back) continue straight ahead and in 20m come to the sign which says 'Pico Ruivo a Encumeada cerca 16km'. To the left of it a reddish-brown path leads down the northwest flank of Pico Ruivo. To the south beautiful views soon open up down into the Nuns' Valley and at the western edge the landscape is dominated by Pico Grande.

After a lot of ascent and descent you come to a fork 1¼ hrs after the sign. Curral das Freiras is down to the left, but you choose the right hand fork with a gentle incline. Soon afterwards a well-trodden path branches off left towards a small clearing where it's possible to camp. Now follows a steep descent, protected with a wire cable, on the northern side of the ridge. The steps of the path can be slippery when wet. You should also be careful after the steps where the path narrows to a partly overgrown and very precipitous mule track.

After a steep ascent the path changes over again to the Curral side. At the crossroads at **Boca das Torrinhas** (1449m) a forest of signs awaits you – the path goes down left at an acute angle to Curral (walk 37) and to the right there's a dilapidated path to Boaventura. After a stop for a picnic go up some steps to a height of almost 1700m, to **Pico do Jorge**, from where there's another fabulous view of the highest peaks.

Now begins the long descent to the Encumeada pass with an impressive view all the way across the São Vicente valley over to the coastal rocks of Porto Moniz in the furthest northwest. In clear weather you catch a glimpse of the wind turbines on the Paúl da Serra plateau.

After a first gate the path, badly eroded in places, runs along the foot of a huge rock face and the view soon opens up of the Ribeira Brava basin. A few minutes after the second gate you can see the transmitter masts on the Encumeada pass for the first time.

Take another rest with wonderful views at an overhanging rock with a bench below and then continue the descent down many steps to the pass. The steps turn into a gravel path along which you descend right down to the road at the **Encumeada pass** (1004m). The bus stop is at the *Encumeada snack-bar*.

Impressive waymarker – the upright Pico Grande.

31 From Eira do Serrado to Curral das Freiras

A descent with a bird's eye view

Eira do Serrado – Curral das Freiras

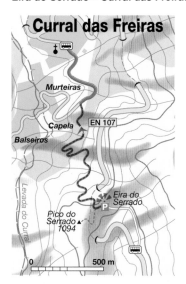

Starting point/return: No. 81 bus from Funchal as far as the Eiro do Serrado bus stop, from there on the cobbled road for a kilometre on foot to the Eira do Serrado viewpoint, 1094m. If you come by car you can park here and go by bus from Curral das Freiras (640m) to the Eira do Serrado bus stop and return along the cobbled road to the car.

Walking time: Eira do Serrado – Curral das Freiras 1 hr 10 min.

Descent: 450m.

Grade: steep descent on a cobbled path almost all of the way.

Refreshment: snack-bar in Eira do Serrado; Nuns Valley restaurant in Curral das Freiras.

Linking tip: if you have a good head for heights you can combine this walk with walk 32. After the cobbled path in walk 31 meets the road, follow the road for about 1km downhill until the Levada do Curral crosses the road.

Many old paths lead down into the Nuns' Valley which up until a few years ago was not linked to the road network. The cobbled path from Eira do Serrado is the shortest and certainly at the start, the most spectacular approach into this basin-shaped valley as well.

Before you begin the descent you should not miss the imposing panorama from the **Eira do Serrado** viewpoint. Follow the steps for 5 minutes from the car park past the souvenir shops up to the viewing platform.

Back at the car park, steps lead 5m from the 'Eira do Serrado 1094m' sign down into a chestnut wood and then soon turn into a cobbled path. As soon as the wood thins out there's an open view of the road to Curral, looking as if it's stuck to the steep rock face.

The path winds downhill so that you quickly reach the road level. The rock projection at the transmitter masts offers an exposed place to stop for a rest. The path gets narrower and for a short while, the bends get tighter and

ESPECIALIDADES

Sopa de Tomate
Sopa de Peixe

•

Peixe fresco todos os dias

•

Espada à Chefe
Bife de Espadarte grelhado

•

Paella à Valenciana
Arroz de Marisco
Ameijoas na Cataplana
Ameijoas Bolhão Pato
Gambas à Indiana
Fragateira
Ovas de Espada
Esparguete à "Jango"
Bife à "Jango"

O Jango
restaurante

servimo
we serv
est

O Jango

restaurante

Rua de Santa Maria, 164 - 166
Tel./ Fax: 291 221 280 - Móvel 91 9918898
9050-040 Funchal - Madeira

steeper. Once above the village roofs, keep left after a short ascent and eventually meet the EN 107. Following this uphill for 10 minutes you will reach the **Curral das Freiras** church where the bus stop is situated.

The road down to Curral das Freiras is just as spectacular as the hiking path.

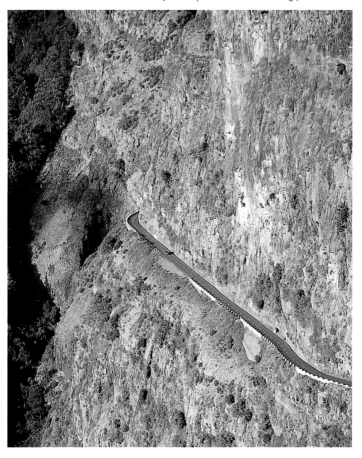

32 Levada do Curral

A detour for those with a good head for heights

Curral das Freiras – waterfall and back

Starting point: from Funchal by car or No. 81 bus into the centre of Curral das Freiras, 640m.

Walking time: Curral das Freiras – waterfall 1 hr 20 min, return 1 hr 20 min. Total time 2 hrs 40 min.

Descent: 100m, the same in ascent.

Grade: the walk is only recommended to those who are totally sure-footed and have a good head for heights. For most of the time you are walking along the small, 25cm wide levada wall. Precipitous places are not protected and you need to go round several waterfalls on narrow paths. It's very slippery when wet and there's a danger of rock fall. You must definitely break the walk at the given place. Landslides and waterfalls make this walk often impassable in winter.

Refreshment: Nuns Valley restaurant in Curral das Freiras.

The Levada do Curral down to Funchal, already constructed in the 16th century, is one of the most impressive, but also most dangerous paths on Madeira. The channel flows right across the middle of the towering rock faces of the Curral river gorge.

From **Curral das Freiras** village follow the road for about 20 minutes down the valley towards Lombo Chão until the *Levada do Curral* crosses the road. Go along the channel in the direction of the flow of water and immediately there's a red sign warning you of how dangerous the path is.

Knotty chestnut and eucalyptus trees cling to the steep slope. The levada forces its way through rocks which you can go round on a path. Soon afterwards the channel disappears for 50m. The valley slopes ahead are getting closer together and far down below the Ribeira do Curral has carved a gorge through the mountains. Now comes the first of the unprotected sections and you reach a tunnel with a **waterfall** plunging over it into the valley.

The tunnel is only about 8m long, but there are bends in the middle and it is dark so that a torch is an advantage to help you over the usually slippery path.

The levada disappears again for a short while. A quarter of an hour after the waterfall you come to a very wet place which you can get round on a path. If you were to continue you would have to scramble 3m up the slippery slope to the levada, but this is where you turn round.

The walk on to *Fajã* is certainly spectacular, but extremely dangerous. On this section of the path there have already been several fatal accidents. If you have enjoyed the levada you can follow it from the Funchal side more safely for a short way (walk 1).

The Levada do Curral flows down to Funchal, but the path is dangerous.

33 From Corticeiras into the Nuns' Valley

The chestnut tree path over Lovers' Pass

Corticeiras – Boca dos Namorados – Curral das Freiras

Starting point: No. 96 bus from Funchal to Corticeiras, 750m.
Return: No. 81 bus from Curral das Freiras.
Walking time: Corticeiras – Boca dos Namorados ¾ hr, Boca dos Namorados – Lombo Chão 1¼ hrs, Lombo Chão – Curral das Freiras 1 hr. Total time 3 hrs.
Ascent: 600m, the same in descent.
Grade: demanding mountain walk with steep ascents and descents on partly stony and slippery paths when wet. There are no really precipitous sections but you need to be totally sure-footed. The walk is also possible in winter when the weather's good.
Refreshment: Nuns Valley restaurant in Curral das Freiras.

The panoramic path over Lovers' Pass was once the most important link from the south coast into the isolated Nuns' Valley. The walk is especially picturesque in autumn when the leaves of the sweet chestnut trees turn a golden red.

The bus stops in **Corticeiras** at a transformer tower. There's a small bar opposite. From the transformer tower go a few metres back along the road and turn left onto the road with the sign 'Boca dos Namorados'. Go left at the fork after 3 minutes and the road narrows and is paved.

On the right hand side you soon pass the gate of the *Quinta Mis Muchachos*. 10m after the Quinta follow the sign left steeply uphill towards an eucalyptus wood. The path is not clear at first as new terraces have been constructed. Keep going straight uphill, looking all the time for the old cobbles.

You cross over an earth road and 10 minutes later you are at **Boca dos Namorados** (1060m), Lovers' Pass. From the wooden fence there's already an impressive view through the trees of Curral situated in the basin-shaped

Nuns' Valley.

valley. At mid-height you can make out the electricity pylon on Pico do Cedro, the destination for the next stage.

On the pass you meet the earth road again. Keep left at the wooden fence and when this finishes an earth track goes downhill. The path may sometimes be submerged in scree and leaves. Zigzagging downhill you reach the **Pico do Cedro** rock spur at the electricity pylon – in fine weather it's one of the most peaceful places on the island to stop for a rest.

You come to a concrete path below the first houses in the valley. Cross a streambed full of basket willows and follow the concrete path uphill to reach the first houses. At a turn-off keep left up the steps and after a few paces you reach the end of the new road in **Lombo Chão**. You could finish the walk here and wait for the bus.

The road brings you round some bends down into the valley bottom. You cross a bridge over the stony riverbed of the Ribeira do Curral. Follow the road uphill and after the first right hand bend climb up the old steps to Curral das Freiras. You cross over the road twice in the next 10 minutes. The third time you meet the *Levada do Curral* running diagonally under the road (walk 32).

Going up the road to the left you pass 8 letterboxes after 200m. Go left here down the steps and after 25m you are on the old cobbled path again which heads straight for the **Curral das Freiras** village church (640m). The taxi rank and the bus stop are near the church on the village road.

34 From Boca da Corrida to Curral das Freiras

Descent over the Donkey Pass into the Nuns' Valley

Boca da Corrida – Boca do Cerro – Curral das Freiras

Starting point: car park at Boca da Corrida forestry house, 1235m.
Getting there and back: the No. 96 bus goes from Funchal via Estreito da Câmara de Lobos as far as Jardim da Serra. From there you have to go the last 3km on foot to Boca da Corrida, so it's best to take a taxi from Estreito da Câmara de Lobos to Boca da Corrida (there's a large taxi rank at the church). Return from Curral das Freiras on No. 81 bus.
Walking time: Boca da Corrida – Boca do Cerro 1 hr, Boca do Cerro – Fajã Escura 1½ hrs, Fajã Escura – Curral das Freiras ½ hr. Total time 3 hrs.
Ascent: 200m, 800m in descent.
Grade: a comfortable broad path as far as Boca do Cerro, then a steep descent. Be very careful when wet.
Sure-footedness and a lack of vertigo essential.
Refreshment: Nuns' Valley restaurant in Curral das Freiras.
Linking tip: this walk can be combined with an ascent of Pico Grande (walk 35).

The walk begins on an easy path with impressive views down into the basin-shaped valley of Curral and up to Pico Grande. From the Donkey Pass, once used a lot by pack animals, a steep path runs down through dense chestnut woods to the Curral river.

From the car park at **Boca da Corrida** forestry house first follow the cobbled path up from the chapel for 15m. A concrete track goes up left between two posts, but keep straight ahead and climb steeply up eight steps. After just under 10 minutes you have a wonderful view of Pico Grande towering up ahead and below, on the right, lies your destination of Curral das Freiras in the valley.

The path crosses over onto the other side of the ridge, now with a view of the Encumeada pass, and in fine weather you can make out the wind turbines on the Paúl da Serra plateau. Back on the Curral side again you pass Boca dos Corgos notch and you climb up to the Passo de Ares. Continue round a wide bend on the flank of Pico do Serradinho (1442m).

At **Boca do Cerro** (1300m), Donkey Pass, the path crosses from the east to the west side. At an orange-coloured board with three stars you come to a turn-off (straight ahead goes to the Encumeada, walk 36). Climb up steeply right on a path for a few metres to a gate on the ridge. 15m after that the path forks. Left goes up to Pico Grande (walk 35), but you go straight on gradually downhill where a red board warns you of the steep descent to Curral. At first it's only moderately steep, but the path, in places very precipitous and unprotected, soon zig-zags down to a conspicuous rock projection which you walk across as if on a bridge.

Curral das Freiras at the foot of the central massif.

Now and then the view opens up through the chestnut wood onto the road bridge far below in Fajã Escura which is the point where you reach the valley bottom. Keep right at two turn-offs, then go straight on.

Half an hour after the rock projection you come to a gate. About 7 minutes after that the path splits into several paths. Keep left and the path soon goes steeply down a slope. Do not go towards the terraced fields at the turn-off, but go straight ahead steeply downhill.

5 minutes later you come to a levada in the village of **Fajã Escura**. Go down the steps lined with lanterns which brings you to the road through the houses. The path is marked with red dots. Cross the streambed on a wooden bridge parallel to the road. 2 minutes later you've reached the village road and down left you come to the bridge over the Ribeira do Curral das Freiras which you saw from above. The bus stop is just behind the bridge. If you do not want to wait for a bus go along the road to the right and in 30 minutes you reach the **Curral das Freiras** church.

35 Pico Grande, 1654m

Striking summit walk with an alpine character

Boca da Corrida – Boca do Cerro – Pico Grande and back

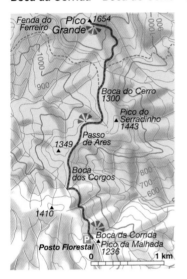

Starting point: by car via Estreito da Câmara de Lobos and Jardim da Serra to the car park on Boca da Corrida, 1235m.

Walking time: Boca da Corrida – Boca do Cerro 1 hr, Boca do Cerro – Pico Grande ¾ hr, return 1¾ hrs. Total time 3½ hrs.

Ascent: 500m, the same in descent.

Grade: this very demanding high mountain walk should only be undertaken on clear days – route-finding in the summit area can be extremely difficult if the mist gathers. Some climbing experience is needed for the last few metres up to the top.

Refreshment: no facilities on the way.

Combination tip: if you do not need to return to your car, descend to Curral das Freiras after climbing Pico Grande (walk 34) or walk to the Encumeada pass (walk 36).

Height-wise, Pico Grande is not in the Top Ten of Madeira walks, but in relation to the degree of difficulty of the ascent and the quality of its views it certainly belongs to the best of them. The mountain, sitting on top of a huge plinth, has fascinating tufa formations in the summit area shaped by wind and water.

From the car park at **Boca da Corrida** forestry house first follow the cobbled path up from the chapel for 15m. A concrete track leads uphill to the left between two posts, but keep going straight ahead and, as in walk 34, climb up to **Boca do Cerro**. There you come to a turn-off at an orange-coloured board with three stars. Climb up right for a few metres on the steep path to the ridge and go through a gate. 15m afterwards the path forks: straight on goes down to Curral (walk 34), the ascent of Pico Grande starts on the left.

Leave the sheep pens on the left and before a temporary hut go up some tracks on the left, indistinct first. Above the hut a red sign warns of the difficult ascent. The path goes past a shelter cut into the rock and seems to finish after 15m, but a *wire cable* fixed to a karabiner now signals the most diffi-

The rocky castle in the Pico Grande summit area.

cult part of the ascent. You ascend the bare rock, hand over hand on the wire cable, for about 15m. 2 minutes later there's another tricky bit, then you go up some steps over uneven rock to a lovely vantage point where Curral das Freiras appears as if laid out on a plate before you. The violet candle-shaped flowers of the Echium candicens blossom here in summer – this endemic plant is called 'Pride of Madeira' by the locals.

The path bends to the left and at first red spots help with the route finding. After some steps, cut into the rock like a staircase, go through a fence and then, exposed in places, the path zigzags towards three solitary sweet chestnut trees.

The path goes below the trees and shortly afterwards crosses a streambed. Discreetly placed red dots and a few cairns help you over this more or less clearly visible path above some smooth rock slabs. Keep heading towards the rocky castle with triple towers ahead.

At the foot of this pitted rock formation, you come again to three sweet chestnut trees and the path goes along the wall on the left up to the summit which looks as if two horns have been placed on top. Below the summit go across a patch of meadow, come to a wire cable over a gully and after a short climbing interlude you are standing on the summit of **Pico Grande**.

36 From Boca da Corrida to Boca da Encumeada, 1004m

Traversing the passes on an old pilgrims' path at the foot of Pico Grande

Boca da Corrida – Boca do Cerro – Boca da Encumeada

Starting point: car park at Boca da Corrida forestry house, 1235m.
Getting there and back: the No. 96 bus goes from Funchal via Estreito da Câmara de Lobos as far as Jardim da Serra. From there you have to go the last 3km on foot to Boca da Corrida, so it's best to take a taxi from Estreito da Câmara de Lobos to Boca da Corrida (there's a large taxi rank at the church).
Return from the Encumeada pass with No. 6 bus.
Walking time: Boca da Corrida – Boca do Cerro 1 hr, Boca do Cerro – Fenda do Ferreiro ¾ hr, Fenda do Ferreiro – Ribeira do Poço 1 hr, Ribeira do Poço – Boca da Encumeada 1¼ hrs. Total time 4 hrs.
Descent: 500m and 300m in ascent.
Grade: at first on a broad path, then on a sometimes narrow and, in summer, wet mule track. The path is at times overgrown with blackberry briars so you are advised to wear long trousers.
There's the danger of stone fall in the Pico Grande area.
Refreshment: Encumeada snack-bar and Encumeada hotel at the end of the walk.

The Encumeada pass is the eye of the needle between the south and the north side of the island and at the same time forms a weather divide where the clouds boil over from the north like unwatched milk. Before there was a road, the old pilgrims' path between Câmara de Lobos and São Vicente was much used. Except for the spectacular section at the foot of the steep rock face of Pico Grande the path is still in good shape today. In places it can be wet and for this reason the walk is better in the summer months.
From the car park at **Boca da Corrida** at the forestry house follow the cobbled path going up from the chapel for 15m. On the left a concrete track goes up between two posts, but keep straight ahead and climb up eight steep steps. After just under 10 minutes you have a marvellous view of Pico Grande towering up ahead. Below right, in the basin-shaped valley lies Curral and in the west you can see the EN 104 going up to the Encumeada pass. In fine weather you can see the wind turbines on the Paúl da Serra plateau.
Go past Boca dos Corgos notch and up to the Passo de Ares. The path goes round a wide bend on the flank of Pico do Serradinho (1443m).
At **Boca do Cerro** go past an orange-coloured board with three stars at the turn-offs to Curral and up to Pico Grande. Continue straight ahead as close

The path runs directly beneath the steep rock face of Pico Grande and is usually slippery even in summer.

as you can to the rock face of Pico Grande. Sometimes you have to climb over scree slopes. The mule track is narrow, overgrown and mostly wet to muddy, but without the bramble bushes at the side of the path it would be precipitous as well. As soon as you walk away from the base of the mountain the path improves and goes to a small vantage point on the rock projection **Fenda do Ferreiro**.

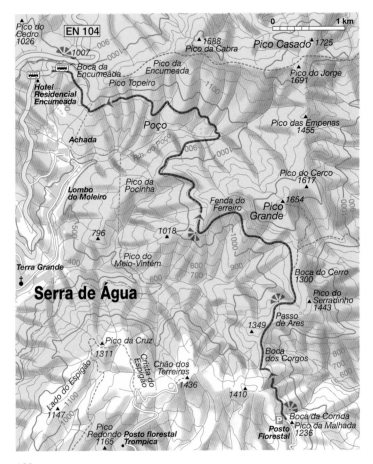

Destination for this delightful walk is the Encumeada pass high above the Ribeira Brava basin.

The path bends round here at a right angle and descends into the Ribeira do Poço valley. Take no notice of any of the paths turning off left in the valley. Already a long way down cross a wooden bridge and shortly afterwards, at a height of about 800m, cross the **Ribeira do Poço** on a stone bridge.

Beneath a dense roof of leaves the path swings out of the valley again and you cross another riverbed. The valley is full of lush green foliage with water bubbling everywhere. As soon as the wood opens out there are impressive views back to the central massif and in the south you can see into the Ribeira Brava basin.

At a conspicuous place where an eucalyptus tree has spread its roots across the path, there's a fork. Left goes down to Serra de Água. Keeping height you go diagonally right. After a small waterfall the path goes along under a pipe which supplies water to the power station in the valley. You can see the transmitter masts on the Encumeada pass above and on the left the Hotel Residencial Encumeada.

After another waterfall you come to a stony roadway which brings you to the EN 104. You can either go 500m uphill to reach the bus stop on **Boca da Encumeada** or 700m downhill to the Hotel Residencial Encumeada where the bus stops as well.

37 From Boca da Encumeada to Curral das Freiras

Descent over the Torrinhas pass into the Nuns' Valley

Boca da Encumeada – Boca das Torrinhas – Fajã Escura

Starting point: Encumeada snack-bar on Boca da Encumeada, 1004m.
No. 6 bus from Funchal to the Encumeada.
Return: from Curral das Freiras back to Funchal with No. 81 bus.
Walking time: Boca da Encumeada – Boca das Torrinhas 2¼ hrs, Boca das Tor-

rinhas – Fajã Escura 1¾ hrs. Total time 4 hrs.
Ascent: 700m, 1100 in descent.
Grade: steep ascent and descent on partly stony path. The walk is marked with yellow and red diamond-shaped signs.
Refreshment: Encumeada snack-bar at the start, restaurant in Curral das Freiras.

The mountain path over the Torrinhas pass is one of the classic link paths into the Curral basin. At the crossroads you come to the paths leading up to Pico Ruivo and down to the north coast. Knotty tree heathers and the smell of ethereal eucalyptus oil accompany you on the descent into the Nuns' Valley.

From **Boca da Encumeada** bus stop at the Encumeada snack-bar follow the EN 104 towards São Vicente and after the next bend turn right onto the gravel track sign-posted 'Pico Ruivo'. The track soon goes right and up to the transmitter masts, but you go straight ahead along the narrow path. A

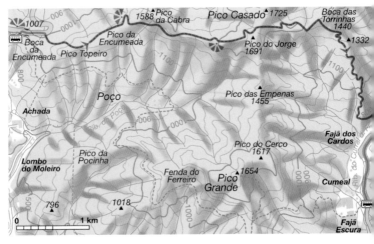

Fajã dos Cardos in the Nuns' Valley.

few metres after the fork you have reached the steps up the ridge path to Pico Ruivo.

The elaborately laid path goes a good one and a half hours up to *Pico do Jorge* with wonderful views of the São Vicente valley and the central massif ahead. Just before the pass keep left at a fork. You eventually come to an exposed rock projection and the descent begins shortly afterwards.

After an ascent through a gap in the rocks you can see down into the basin-shaped valley of Curral for the first time. Steps leads down to where the paths cross over at **Boca das Torrinhas**. Leave the ridge path here to go right for the start of the descent to Curral. The path zigzags down through heather. A path joins from above left before you come to an eucalyptus wood. Fallen tree trunks lie strewn across the path. Only now and again you can catch a glimpse through the wood of the terraced fields of Fajã dos Cardos in the valley.

The descent gets steeper and the path goes through an eroded gully to meet a parallel path coming from above which you continue to follow downhill to the left. The wood is now behind you and you cross a levada channel to reach the first terraces and some sheds covered in corrugated iron. The path narrows to a rough track, but the yellow and red waymarkings help you find your way through the farmland criss-crossed with paths.

You pass a station for measuring rainfall which has a fence round it. 10 minutes later you cross the Ribeira do Curral over a bridge and meet the road Fajã dos Cordos – Curral. Following the road to the right for one kilometre you come to the bus stop at the bridge in **Fajã Escura**.

If you do not want to wait for the bus, continue straight on to the centre of **Curral das Freiras**, two kilometres away.

Paúl da Serra and west Madeira

The Boca de Encumeada divides Madeira into an eastern and western half and from the top of the pass you can see the north as well as the south coast. From Encumeada there's a road going up to **Paúl da Serra**, for Madeira an unexpectedly flat plateau.

Paúl doesn't stand for a man's name, but means marsh in Portuguese. In fact the plain, between 1400 and 1600m high and usually enveloped in clouds, reminds you of a high Scottish moor. Seemingly endless meadows of moss and fern are used as pasture-land for sheep and cows. After winter rainfall basins turn into small lakes, mountain rivers emerge and cascade as waterfalls into the valley. Levadas channel the precious water down to the farmland in the coastal areas. This 100sq.km. area is uninhabited and offers the walker uninterrupted peace and solitude.

A sea-water pool in Porto Moniz: waiting for the waves to come crashing over.

Porto Moniz lies peacefully in the furthest northwest.

The most well-known walking region on Madeira is **Rabaçal** at the western edge of Paúl da Serra. Here you can wonder at the effervescent waterfalls, tree heathers, laurel trees hanging with beardmoss and thick pillows of moss along fairy tale levada paths. The levadas have been constructed on three levels, as it were, and are linked to one another by mountain paths and steps.

Since access from the tourist centres Funchal and Caniço to Rabaçal and to the north coast in particular is too far for a day trip, you are advised to find a base in the west for a few days at least. Accommodation in the rural **Prazeres** is well-placed for walkers and nature lovers. The comfortable 4-star Hotel Jardim Atlântico, (tel 291820220) has made a name for itself with its environmentally friendly hotel management. In **Porto Moniz** in the most north-western corner of the island you can find accommodation which is good value for money, but the village is only recommended in summer due to the days being cool and overcast in winter. A particular plus is the fact that Porto Moniz has by far the most beautiful sea-water pool on the island. And when the daytrippers start making their way back in the late afternoon, a tranquillity descends on the place with a sunset usually to oneself.

38 Botanising in the Folhadal

Along the Levada do Norte to the Lily-of-the-Valley trees

Boca da Encumeada – Folhadal and back

Starting point: by car or No. 6 bus to the Encumeada pass.
Walking time: Boca da Encumeada – Folhadal ¾ hr, return ¾ hr. Total time 1½ hrs.
Ascent: negligible.
Grade: easy levada walk. There's one tunnel which is long and some precipitous places are not protected.

Refreshment: Encumeada snack-bar at the start.
Alternative route: follow the Levada das Rabaçal straight ahead at the fork in front of the first tunnel. After ¾ hr you reach a long tunnel which goes to the Cascalho. From there you could climb up to Cristo Rei (walk 41 in reverse).

The Lily-of-the-Valley tree is called Folhada in Madeira (clethra arborea) which casts a spell over the mountain region with its splendid flowers in late summer. Laurel trees, Juniper, Hydrangea, white and blue flowering Lilies of the Nyle, wild Orchids and Shrubby Sea Blite serrated like dandelions make walking the path a botanical lesson.

Opposite the snack-bar on the **Encumeada pass** there's a yellow sign for 'Folhadal' pointing up the steps to the *Levada do Norte*. Follow the broad channel upstream. You soon have a beautiful view to the south east of Pico Grande. After 6 minutes you reach a tunnel in front of which the levada branches off. Go right, through the tunnel which is about 600m long. The first 30 to 40m are relatively narrow and low so that you have to crouch down slightly. The rest of the tunnel is easy going, especially as you can see the end of the tunnel.

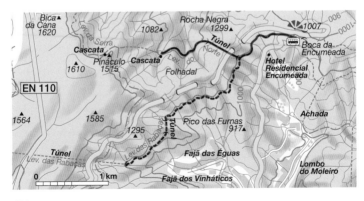

The 'two-lane' Levada do Norte to the Folhadal.

After the tunnel there are some precipitous places to overcome, not all protected with a fence. The vegetation is extremely luxuriant in the **Folhadal**. Bracken and Hydrangeas arch deeply over the levada, moss and Maidenhair fern grow along the channel and finger-long trout dart about in the water. Through the green jungle you can catch a glimpse of the São Vicente valley.

3 minutes after a short tunnel you come to a long tunnel where a sizeable waterfall plunges down into the valley in front of it. You turn round here and go the same way back.

39 From Bica da Cana to the Pináculo

To the sugar loaf mountain of Madeira

Bica da Cana – Levada da Serra – Pináculo and back

Starting point: by car to Bica da Cana (1580m) on the EN 110 between the Encumeada pass and Paúl da Serra.
Walking time: Bica da Cana – Pináculo ¾ hr, return ¾ hr. Total time 1½ hrs.

Descent: a good 50m, the same in ascent.
Grade: at times quite narrow and stony, most of the year wet and slippery.
Refreshment: no facilities on the way.

Not only Rio, but also Madeira has a sugar loaf mountain even though the Pináculo is no more than a miniature version of its famous Brazilian brother. This short walk is extremely worthwhile especially in the summer months – in winter sometimes the path can be very slippery.

The starting point is **Bica da Cana** on the En 110. Near the entrance to the mountain hut with its boundary of concrete posts go left onto a grassy path and keep heading towards a fence about 25m away. Follow the path left along the fence and go over a gate at a stile. Afterwards keep going diagonally left through a heather tunnel. The now rocky path descends gently and may be overgrown with ferns.

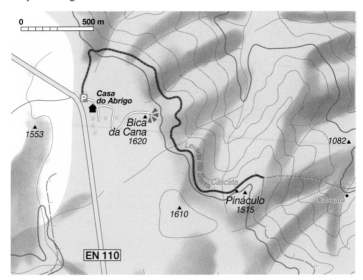

Pináculo (on the right) with a backdrop of the central massif.

After a good 10 minutes go left at a fork and 2 minutes later another path crosses over which you follow to the right. At first keeping your height, then going gradually uphill, the path soon goes through tree heather beside a rocky wall and the slope falls away steeply down to the left. At a clearing you can see the Pináculo ahead (1515m) and behind that the highest peaks on Madeira. Above you the wind turbines of Paúl da Serra are turning in the wind.

The well-trodden mule track maintains height and keeps heading towards the sugar loaf mountain. Everywhere there's the dripping and splashing of water and soon the **Levada da Serra**, fed by a small waterfall, runs alongside. At the sign 'Casa de Abrigo do Carmujo' continue straight ahead and now the most spectacular part of the walk lies in front of you. Like a rim between wall and slope the path goes round a semi-circular wall of basalt. Part of the path has broken away – be careful because a small waterfall makes walking round it slippery. Just afterwards a big waterfall rushes into the levada and you can sometimes get quite wet from the spray.

Pináculo is not very far away now and at the foot of the sugar loaf mountain there's a good place to stop for a rest and to camp in front of the imposing backdrop of the central massif.

40 The fern path onto Pico Ruivo do Pául, 1640m

Onto the highest mountain of Paúl da Serra with beautiful views

Estanquinhos turn-off – Pico Ruivo do Paúl and back

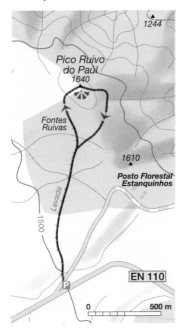

Starting point: coming from the Encumeada pass you turn off sharp right from the EN 110, 2km after Bica da Cana, onto a road sign-posted to the Estanquinhos forestry house, 1520m.
Park at the side of the road immediately after the turn-off.

Walking time: Estanquinhos turn-off – Pico Ruivo do Paúl 35 min, return 35 min. Total time just under 1¼ hrs.

Ascent: a good 100m, the same in descent.

Grade: easy walk on a sometimes overgrown path with a short ascent and descent.

Refreshment: no facilities on the way.

The Pico Ruivo do Paúl rises up only a short way out of the meadows of fern on the plateau, but far enough to give a magnificent view in all directions. It's best to take this short walk only on clear days to make it even more beautiful.

At the **Estanquinhos turn-off** follow the 15cm wide levada channel which heads straight for the summit. Through the emerald green meadows of ferns in summer you come past a small cluster of trees and into a small light pine wood. Cross over a stony roadway and shortly afterwards you come to the source of the levada. Again through dense bracken you climb up in a straight line to the four-sided trig point on **Pico Ruivo do Paúl**. A fabulous panorama over the plateau and the wind farm and of the central massif with Arieiro, Torres and Pico Grande awaits you.

For the **return** go from the trig point parallel to the fence in a northerly direction towards the wind turbines. On the left hand side the plateau drops away steeply into the São Vicente valley.

Descend to the visible path running across the base of the Pico. At the foot of the mountain follow the broad meadow path to the right, first leaving the little wood on your right and then meeting a cross path which you follow to the right downhill into the pine wood. There you meet the levada again which brings you back left to the starting point.

Bracken covers the Paúl da Serra in a green carpet.

41 From Cristo Rei to Cascalho

Along the levada da Bica da Cana into the basin-shaped valley

Cristo Rei – Cascalho and back

Starting point: coming from the Encumeada pass drive along the EN 110 to Paúl da Serra, turn left 4.5km after Bica da Cana onto the EN 209 and after 3km reach the statue of Christ (1320m). There's no public transport.

Walking time: Cristo Rei – Levada da Bica da Cana turn-off 40 min, turn-off – Cascalho 1 hr 10 min, return 1 hr 50 min. Total time 3 hrs 40 min.

Descent: a good 500m, the same in ascent.

Grade: descent along a track and the rest of the way along a precipitous levada. Danger of rock fall in the basin-shaped valley. A torch is useful in the tunnel.

Refreshment: no facilities on the way.

Alternative route: from the end of the walk you can continue through a long tunnel to the Encumeada pass (see alternative in walk 38). Don't forget replacement batteries for your torch!

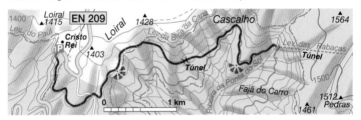

The walk begins as a gentle levada walk from where you descend along a supply path to the channel system of Cascalho. Your objective is a huge basin-shaped valley with vertical rock faces and rushing waterfalls.

From the car park at the **Cristo Rei** go down the EN 209. After a right hand bend the narrow *Levada da Bica da Cana* crosses the road after 4 minutes and you follow this to the left. After a good 20 minutes you come past a picnic spot and cross over a cobbled road.

On the other side of the road you go up the slope along the levada and soon you are able to see a path going into the valley. But before that, walk for a quarter of an hour along the levada at the upper edge of the valley, at times only along a small 30cm wide channel wall. At the aforementioned track you reach the **turn-off for the Levada da Bica da Cana**. Now leave the levada to go into the valley. A new water channel accompanies you now on the left of the path and is fed by many rivulets draining from the hillside. Down below you can see the village of Lombada perched on an exposed mountain ridge.

You come to a dark tunnel. Be careful, as the levada crosses the path in the middle. 10 minutes after the tunnel a waterfall plunges into the levada from almost 100m. The view now opens out into the semi-circular basin-shaped valley. On the left you pass a tunnel and a water house cut into the rock. From now on continue along the levada wall which is protected with a fence and circumnavigate the impressive **Cascalho**. Dozens of small and large waterfalls plunge down the vertical rock face.

From Cascalho you can follow the levada into the neighbouring basin, negotiating several unprotected sections in the process. The second basin may not be so huge, but it is no less beautiful. Turn round before the long tunnel.

In front of the impressive basin-shaped valley of Cascalho.

42 From Cristo Rei to the Fátima chapel

Stroll through the sea of ferns on Paúl da Serra

Cristo Rei – Rabaçal road and back

Starting point: coming from the Encumeada pass drive up the EN 110 to Paúl da Serra and 4.5km after Bica da Cana turn off left onto the EN 209 which brings you to the Statue of Christ after 3km (1320m).
Walking time: Cristo Rei – Nossa Senhora de Fátima chapel 1¼ hrs, return 1¼ hrs. Total time 2½ hrs.

Ascent: negligible.
Grade: easy walk on a narrow levada path.
Refreshment: no facilities on the way.
Linking tip: the very beautiful levada walk into the Ribeira Grande valley (walk 43) begins at the end of the walk on the other side of the EN 110.

The *Levada do Paúl* runs along the edge of the Paúl da Serra plateau through beautiful meadows of fern interspersed with yellow Gorse. Grazing cows are often the only sign of civilization here. In clear visibility you have a wonderful view of the south coast lying 1200m below.

From the car park at **Cristo Rei** follow the EN 209 downhill. After a right hand bend the narrow *levada* crosses the road after 4 minutes and you follow this to the right downstream. A narrow path runs along the channel, only 20cm wide, through what seems to be an endless sea of ferns which cover the slopes in a wash of olive green to rust colours in late summer.

After half an hour cross a stream with a small waterfall and shortly afterwards you can just see the Pico da Urze hotel above. The levada again runs

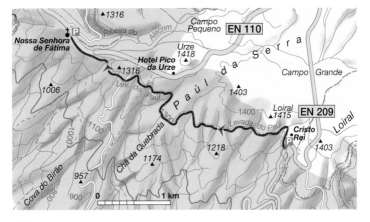

The uninhabited Paúl da Serra plateau is only used as grazing land.

across a streambed and a secondary levada flows in from the side. You go past some caves which are dug into the hillside and the path here is very narrow. You meet the EN 110 at the inconspicuous **Nossa Senhora de Fátima chapel**. Following this to the left you come to the **Rabaçal turn-off** after 100m where a colourful market for souvenirs is held on weekdays in good weather.

43 Into the Ribeira Grande valley

Picturesque trip to the trout pond at the 'big river'

Rabaçal turn-off – Ribeira Grande and back

Starting point: car park on the EN 110 at the turn-off to Rabaçal, 1278m.
Walking time: Rabaçal turn-off – Ribeira Grande 1 hr, return 1 hr. Total time 2 hrs.
Ascent: negligible.
Grade: gentle levada walk with a few mildly precipitous sections.
Refreshment: no facilities on the way.

The Ribeira Grande is one of many source rivers in the marshy highlands of Paúl da Serra. A dream of a walk through heather and metre high bilberry bushes! There's a marvellous spot to stop for a rest awaiting you at your destination, with a waterfall and a trout pond.

From the car park at the **Rabaçal turn-off** follow the road towards the Rabaçal forestry house about 100m downhill to the first telephone mast. From there a well-trodden path brings you to the levada after 50m which you follow upstream. The often dusty path in summer next to the channel goes through tree heathers in a wide left hand bend round the valley and after 10 minutes crosses the Ribeira do Alecrim at a semi-circular water tank.

Further on the water channel forces its way through rocks where you need to negotiate some moderately precipitous places. Go up some steep steps next to the levada with water rushing downwards to a mountain ridge. Soon you have a beautiful view of the Rabaçal levadas flowing far below and softly rounded hilltops give the highlands a charming character.

The sound of waterfalls gets nearer. You come to the **Ribeira Grande** streambed, filled with smoothly polished rocks, which feeds the levada. Above the source of the levada waterfalls cascade downwards and below the rocks you can see a small trout pond.

The »stairway to heaven« on the way to the trout pond.

44 The Risco waterfall near Rabaçal

Leisurely short walk to the big waterfall

Rabaçal – Risco waterfall and back

Starting point: from Funchal by car via the Encumeada pass and Paúl da Serra to the Rabaçal forestry house, 1064m. The approach road to the forestry house from the EN 110 is windy and extremely narrow – be careful of oncoming traffic! There's no public transport.

Walking time: Rabaçal forestry house – Risco waterfall 25 min, return 25 min. Total

time 50 min.
Ascent: negligible.
Grade: leisurely stroll on a broad sign-posted levada path.
Refreshment: no facilities on the way.
Linking tip: this short walk to the waterfall can be combined with walks 45 and 46 to make a great round-trip.

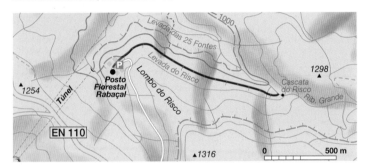

This walk to the 'dangerous waterfall' near Rabaçal is a must for every visitor to Madeira, and as a consequence, the path is much used. From Lagoa do Vento water plunges down a smooth rock face from a height of 100m and doesn't come to rest until another 100m below the path.

From the car park follow the sign posts just in front of the **Rabaçl forestry house** to 'Risco' and '25 Fontes' down into the wood. After 2 minutes you meet the *Levada do Risco* and again there are signs along the now broad and easy path.

At the fork after 4 minutes continue straight ahead (if you want to link walks 45 and 46 go downhill right after viewing the waterfall). Past some small waterfalls you come to another fork after 10 minutes. Follow the levada straight on here and maintaining height beside a fence into a semi-circular basin you are standing in front of the **Risco waterfall** a few minutes later. The path through the tunnels to the left edge of the waterfall is no longer passable (red no-entry sign).

Return the same way.

Rabaçal's 'dangerous waterfall' has little water in summer –
but it's still impressive.

45 From Rabaçal to the 25 springs

Picture book views of nature

Rabaçal – 25 Fontes and back

Starting point: from Funchal by car via the Encumeada pass and Paúl da Serra to the Rabaçal forestry house, 1064m. There is no public transport.
Walking time: Rabaçal forestry house – 25 Fontes 50 min, return 50 min. Total time 1 hr 40 min.
Descent: 100m, the same in ascent.
Grade: you need a good head for heights and to be sure-footed.
Refreshment: no facilities on the way.
Linking tip: from the Levada 25 Fontes you can descend to the Levada da Rocha Vermelha (walk 46).
Alternative route: from the Levada 25 Fontes it's possible to walk down to Loreto on the southwest coast (bus connection). Coming from the Levada Risco follow the Levada 25 Fontes to the left. Shortly after a 800m long tunnel leave the levada at a small bridge and go downhill until you reach the Levada da Rocha Vermelha. Following it to the left till you reach the end of the levada you take the path downhill

and reach the Levada Nova after 20 minutes. Descend left there and after another 40 minutes at a house ruin go down right along a cobbled path to the road and Loreto church. About 2½ hrs from Rabaçal.

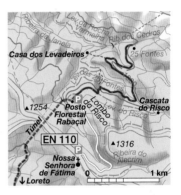

The *Levada of the '25 springs'* is one of the water courses which drains Rabaçal and brings the precious water to the Calheta power station. It is no less famous than the *Levada do Risco* one level above. It doesn't in fact have such a spectacular waterfall, but the romantic channel path through bushes of heather and laurel woods will stand comparison with the most beautiful levada routes on the island.

From the car park follow the signposts just in front of the **Rabaçal forestry house** to 'Risco' and '25 Fontes' down into the wood. After 2 minutes you meet the *Levada do Risco* which you follow for 4 minutes as far as the sign-posted turn-off. At the green board with three stars descend left to the *Levada 25 Fontes*. When you reach the levada continue upstream to the right.

A comfortable path, broad at first, runs next to the levada. The levada disappears for a short while at a pipe. Descend the steps with a protective handrail to the deeply cut gorge of the Ribeira Grande which you cross over on a bridge.

The 25 springs.

On the other side of the gorge steps lead up to the levada again and a water house. Continue straight ahead past the water grills on the now very narrow path. Tree heathers form a closed tunnel roof above your heads and softens the angle of the now very precipitous slope. You can hang on to the hip-high channel wall as if it were a rail.

On a right hand bend, about 10 minutes after the bridge, a well-trodden path turns off left steeply downhill (walk46). Continue following the levada until a channel cascades down from the right in front of a bridge. Following the sign '25 Fontes' you come to the rock basin after 40m where the **25 springs** spill down into the pools in front of the steep rock face made green with ferns. If you want, you can follow the levada for another 10 minutes into the Ribeira dos Cedros valley to its source.

46 Levada da Rocha Vermelha

Long levada round-walk through the fairy tale forest of Rabaçal

Rabaçal – Levada da Rocha Vermelha – Rabaçal

Starting point: from Funchal by car via the Encumeada pass and Paúl da Serra to the Rabaçal forestry house, 1064m. There is no public transport.

Walking time: Rabaçal forestry house – Levada da Rocha Vermelha 1 hr, levada – waterfall 1½ hrs, waterfall – Rabacal forestry house 2 hrs 10 min. Total time 4 hrs 40 min.

Desecent: a good 200m, the same in ascent.

Grade: precipitous sections and steep steps requiring a head for heights and sure-footedness. Slippery when wet.

Refreshment: no facilities on the way.

The walk along the *Levada da Rocha Vermelha* is the longest of the Rabaçal walks, the most demanding and therefore not as popular. The evergreen subtropical vegetation and the distant views into the Ribeira da Janela valley make it a delightfully scenic walk – being able to harvest blackberries in September is a bonus. A sample of unspoiled nature at its finest!

From the car park follow the signposts just in front of the **Rabaçal forestry house** to 'Risco' and '25 Fontes' down into the wood. After 2 minutes you meet the *Levada do Risco* which you follow for 4 minutes to the sign-posted turn-off and then descend left to the *Levada 25 Fontes*. At the levada go upstream right.

After a short way along the channel some steps go down to the bridge over the Ribeira Grande and back up to the levada. 10 minutes after the bridge on a right hand bend a well-trodden path turns off left from the *Levada 25 Fontes* and after a steep descent you reach the **Levada da Rocha Vermelha** at a walnut tree and above a water house.

Following the levada upstream you pass a cave hewn into the rocks. You cross the bridge over the narrow Ribeira dos Cedros ravine. A waterfall rushes down on the right hand side and two streams merge with one another. Immediately after the bridge continue to follow the levada left before the long Seixal tunnel.

The levada now flows in loops round the hillside on the right out of the valley, sometimes under shady tree heathers, sometimes with views deep into the Ribeira da Janela valley. Cross over several overflows while small waterfalls crash down from the slope, and you need to find a way round some slippery and wet narrow sections.

After a good hour on the levada the water channel narrows to 6 inches and you come to some *stone steps* where the water shoots down a narrow groove. Climb up 80m on more than 200 steep steps and be careful in wet weather not to slip.

At the top of the steps keep left on a well-trodden path and soon you meet the levada again and then a magnificent **waterfall**. After heavy rainfall in winter it is difficult to get round this point and it's a good idea to turn back. If it is passable you can follow the levada to its source through a fairy tale wood of heather, negotiating on the way some more unprotected places (1 hour there and back).

Go back along the levada as far as the place at the water house where you descended from the 25 Fontes.

As an alternative for the return follow the levada straight on and after 6 minutes you meet a *concrete bridge* protected with a wire fence.

About 10m after that do not enter the tunnel but turn sharp left uphill. After a few steps the path becomes cobbled and you go steeply up through the wood to the *Levada 25 Fontes*. Continue left at the levada and after 5 minutes climb some steps onto the third level to the *Levada do Risco*. Following this to the right you come back in 10 minutes to the car park at the **Rabaçal forestry house**.

The 'fairy tale wood' on the Levada do Rocha Vermelha.

47 From Prazeres to Calheta

Along the eucalyptus levada through the quiet southwestern valleys

Prazeres – Ribeira da Achada – Calheta

Starting point: main street in Prazeres at the crossroads to the Jardim Atlântico hotel and Paúl da Serra.
Getting there and back: by car or No. 107 bus to Prazeres, 640m. With No. 107 bus from Calheta to Prazeres or Funchal.
Walking time: Prazeres – Atalhinho water house 1¼ hrs, water house – Ribeira da Achada 1 hr, Ribeira da Achada – Calheta 1¾ hrs. Total time 4 hrs.
Descent: a good 300m.
Grade: gentle path, lack of vertigo would be an advantage in a few places.
Refreshment: simple snack-bar in Calheta.

The name is not quite right – the *Levada Nova* is not so new. It was already in use in 1953 and since then has been snaking its way along the south coast for more than 50km. Follow it from Prazeres over countless mountain ridges through eucalyptus woods into isolated valleys to the point just before its 'source', the Calheta hydroelectric power station.

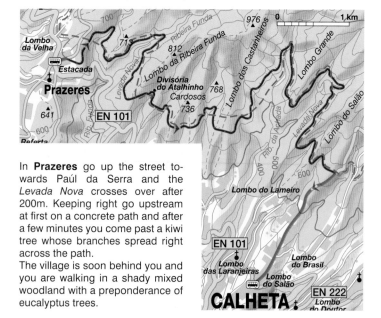

In **Prazeres** go up the street towards Paúl da Serra and the *Levada Nova* crosses over after 200m. Keeping right go upstream at first on a concrete path and after a few minutes you come past a kiwi tree whose branches spread right across the path.
The village is soon behind you and you are walking in a shady mixed woodland with a preponderance of eucalyptus trees.

Prazeres parish church.

The levada flows into the Ribeira Funda valley. Black-charred tree trunks remind you of the last big forest fire in the middle of the nineties. Lilies-of-the-Nyle and Hydrangeas announce the presence of the **Atalhinho water house**. Your path goes straight through a luxuriant garden where apple trees and artichokes, roses and dahlias are lovingly tended by the warden.

The path soon opens out to give you a view of the village of Lombo dos Moinhos and the sea below. After crossing several forest paths and going through a gate the levada flows deep into the Ribeira da Achada valley. On the opposite side of the valley you can just see the path ahead and also enjoy some very beautiful views of the edge of the Paúl da Serra plateau. The further you go into the valley the more picturesque it becomes. Heathers and bracken cover the slopes of Pico Gordo (1264m). There's a nice place to stop for a rest at the **Ribeira da Achada** pools.

Another half hour further on you cross over the *Ribeira do Raposo* and after another 30 minutes you come to a large water tank. Go round the left hand edge. Further along the levada you pass another water house and eventually meet the road coming down from Paúl da Serra. Downhill to the right brings you to Lombo do Salão and the main road in **Calheta**. The bus stop is just round to the right.

48 Paúl do Mar

Long coastal round-walk in the west

Hotel Jardim Atlântico – Paúl do mar – Fajã da Ovelha – Prazeres

Starting point: by car to the Jardim Atlântico hotel, 400m.
If you come by bus get off at the crossroads in Prazeres and follow the road for 1.7km as far as the hotel.
Walking time: Jardim Atlântico hotel – Paúl do Mar 50 min, Paúl do Mar – Fajã da Ovelha 1¾ hrs, Fajã da Ovelha – Levada Nova ¼ hr, Levada Nova – Prazeres

2½ hrs. Total time 5 hrs 20 min.
Descent: 400m, 640m in ascent.
Grade: steep descent and ascent without shade on old cobbled paths, the last section on a gentle levada path.
Take swimwear!
Refreshment: café and restaurant in the Jardim Atlântico hotel, Lagomar restaurant in Paúl do Mar.

You ought to be quite fit for this long round-walk. A steep descent brings you down to the sea into the shabby looking fishing village of Paúl do Mar. The ascent through sparse coastal vegetation is just as steep back up to the *Levada Nova*, along which the walk comes to a leisurely end.

Descent to Paúl do Mar.

20m below the reception for the **Jardim Atlântico hotel** you see a sign 'Vereda Paúl do Mar'. Continue along the road through the apartment blocks and after 30m take the first steps on the right downhill in between two apartment houses and you meet the restored cobbled path. On the left you can look down onto the idyllically situated Jardim do Mar and Paúl do Mar lies by the sea down on the right. The cobbled path winds down steeply. Soon you see the boat mooring where the path reaches the village.

From **Paúl do Mar** harbour go right at first along the promenade beside the water then on the broad village path past the church, the chimneys of the disused fish factory and the football pitch. Below the *Café Bellavista* there's a boat ramp with fishing boats and here in calm seas you can glide into the sea over slippery stones.

50m after the café you cross the bridge over a streambed and go up the concrete track on the right at a transformer house. The cobbled path to Fajã da Ovelha begins after 30m at the last house.

*Bit by bit, nature reclaims something which man has abandoned –
on the Levada Nova.*

A long steep ascent follows through an arid coastal vegetation of Prickly
Pears and agaves. At the viewpoint by the old conveyor belt you can take a
breather and at this point the cape falls away vertically down to the sea.
You can see the Fajã da Ovelha church already above. 10 minutes after the
viewpoint you cross a tarmac road and ascend diagonally right up the narrower village road. The road turns into a concrete track. A cobbled path cuts
across and you follow this up to the right to the church. At **Fajã da Ovelha**
church square go up a few steps, cross over a road and continue uphill
keeping left along the concrete path. The path soon becomes surfaced and
goes past the usually busy village wash house. A few houses of undressed
stone are situated along the path.

A quarter of an hour after the church you meet the **Levada Nova** at a height
of 640m which you follow upstream to the right. The levada snakes it way
through two valleys where agricultural land interchanges with pine forests
and meadows of fern.

After a comfortable hour along the levada it disappears under a cobbled
road. Go 6m up the road to the left and you meet the channel again. 20 minutes later, cross over an asphalt road in *Raposeira*. The levada here runs
through a private garden. Follow the road for about 15m and go round the
house.

The levada crosses several roads from now on. 10 minutes after a water house it flows for a short way beside the EN 101 and then goes for 40m under the road.

After a last short bend into a valley you reach a second water house and the road coming down from Paúl do Serra after that. Leave the levada here and descend 2 minutes down to the main road in **Prazeres**.

The bus stop is at the crossroads. If you have to return to the Jardim Atlântico hotel take a taxi or go the 1.7km on foot.

The splendid yucca is also called Adam's Needle because of its blossom.

49 **Ponta do Pargo**

Tranquil round-walk in the western corner of Madeira

Ponta do Pargo – Levada Nova – Cabo – Ponta do Pargo

Starting point: by car or No. 80 bus to the church square in Ponta do Pargo, 462m.
Walking time: Ponta do Pargo – Pedregal 25 min, Pedregal – Levada Nova 20 min, Levada Nova – Cabo 1¼ hrs, Cabo – Ponta do Pargo 1½ hrs. Total time 3½ hrs.
Ascent: about 200m, the same in descent.
Grade: the narrow path along the levada may be overgrown with ferns in places. The return is on a gentle cobbled path.
Refreshment: Solar do Pero restaurant opposite Ponta do Pargo church.

From Ribeira Brava a windy road goes via Calheta to the western corner of the island. The solitary light house of Ponta do Pargo on the coastal cliff, almost 400m in height, guides ships round the protruding cape. From the village church go up to the *Levada Nova* which winds through primeval meadows of ferns and light pine woods give you clear views of the deep blue sea. A walk which is rarely done, but none the less worthwhile.

At the crossroads at **Ponta do Pargo** church an asphalt road goes down left at the Solar do Pero restaurant to Salão do Baixo and to a 'miradouro'. However, you follow the road straight ahead gently uphill to the next crossroads and at *Bar Malta* continue down the concrete track. The track brings you into a valley and over a bridge on the other side back up to a well in the **Pedregal** part of the town. Where the paths cross 40m after the well branch off right uphill. After a few metres you pass a large chicken farm and shortly afterwards you cross the EN 101. At a little old Madeira house the cobbled path turns into an earth track which brings you up to the levada.

A quarter of an hour after the EN 101 you need be careful not to miss the levada: on the right of the path head towards a metre wide concrete block with a reddish brown iron door and above this you come to the *Levada Nova* (630m), just half a metre wide. Follow it downstream and the channel disappears immediately under an arched bridge.

Light pine woods and bracken border the Levada Nova to Cabo.

Cross over the path coming from above and now along the levada path continue through rich green vegetation.

You have soon gone round two wide valley clefts and the path becomes a rough well-trodden path covered in grass. Once through three more side valleys after just under an hour, cross the EN 101 on the levada. 5 minutes later you meet the road to Cabo. The levada flows into a water tank here. Follow the road left and keeping straight ahead through **Cabo** you reach the solitary *Nossa Senhora da Boa Morte* chapel (450m) below.

From the asphalt car park next to the church follow the earth road which maintains height and contours round a small valley. You come to where the paths cross and the houses of Lombada Velha now lie ahead. It's worth making a short *detour* down to the right to the steep coastline.

The path heads for a small trig point where there's a sheer drop. It's a beautiful place to take a rest if you can find a suitable place to sit – you can see the Ponta do Pargo light house in the southwest.

Back at the crossroads go into **Lombada Velha**. You come to an old cobbled path in the village which, if you keep to the right, brings you down into a valley. Past a small area covered in river gravel and with a date palm, climb straight up to Pedregal and below the hen-house you meet the little asphalt road again, on which you went up to the *Levada Nova* 2½ hours ago. Go straight on and you will pass the well you came to before, then return along the concrete track to **Ponta do Pargo**.

50 From Lamaceiros into the Ribeira da Janela gorge

The showcase levada in the furthest northwest

Lamaceiros – water house and back

Starting point: water house in Lamceiros, 400m. From Porto Moniz follow the EN 101 for about 3km towards Paúl da Serra and turn off left to Lamaceiros at the sign 'Ribeira da Jenela'. Keep straight ahead at a crossroads and eventually reach the water house on the left below the road. You can park here. There is no public transport.

Walking time: Lamaceiros – water house 1 hr 50 min, return 1 hr 50 min. Total time 3 hrs 40 min.

Ascent: negligible.

Grade: easy levada walk, precipitous places are protected. A torch is needed for the long tunnels.

Refreshment: no facilities on the way, good fish restaurants in Porto Moniz.

Alternative route: if you so wish you can follow the levada from the water house through five more tunnels to the entrance of a last one, almost 2km long (another 1½ hrs there and back). The path can be very slippery.

The Ribeira da Janela is the longest river on Madeira. From the source area in Rabaçal it flows down to the northwest coast in rapids. The deeply cut valley with its unspoiled landscape is one of the most beautiful on the island and can easily be reconnoitered from Lamaceiros for a short way along the *Levada da Central da Ribeira da Janela*. There's hardly another levada so well cared for. Hydrangeas and Lilies-of-the-Nyle festoon the path. Picnic benches invite you to take a quiet rest with views of an elaborately terraced landscape – and unusually, there are even litter bins.

Opposite the water house in **Lamaceiros** follow the levada downstream to the right in front of the enormous water tank. After the first right hand bend

you already have an impressive view of the terraced hillside of the Ribeira da Janela valley. The levada makes route-finding easy as it goes deeper and deeper into the valley past apple, peach and maracuja trees. The path gets narrower and then in 7 minutes you go through a tunnel. A second, not quite so long tunnel follows immediately. There's a bend in the middle so that you cannot see the exit. A quarter of an hour later you reach the **water house** and from the terrace there's a beautiful panorama into the upper Ribeira da Janela valley as far as Rabaçal.
Return the same way.

Terraced countryside à la Bali in the Janela valley.

Index